SEA WOLF
OF THE
CONFEDERACY

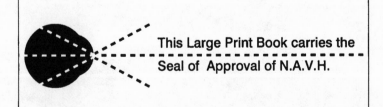

This Large Print Book carries the
Seal of Approval of N.A.V.H.

SEA WOLF
OF THE
CONFEDERACY

The Daring Civil War Raids of
Naval Lt. Charles W. Read

David W. Shaw

Thorndike Press • Waterville, Maine

Published in 2004 by arrangement with
Free Press, an imprint of Simon & Schuster, Inc.

Thorndike Press® Large Print American History.

The tree indicium is a trademark of Thorndike Press.

The text of this Large Print edition is unabridged.
Other aspects of the book may vary from the original edition.

Set in 16 pt. Plantin.

Printed in the United States on permanent paper.

ISBN 0-7862-6700-3 (lg. print : hc : alk. paper)

For the fallen

As the Founder/CEO of NAVH, the only national health agency solely devoted to those who, although not totally blind, have an eye disease which could lead to serious visual impairment, I am pleased to recognize Thorndike Press* as one of the leading publishers in the large print field.

Founded in 1954 in San Francisco to prepare large print textbooks for partially seeing children, NAVH became the pioneer and standard setting agency in the preparation of large type.

Today, those publishers who meet our standards carry the prestigious "Seal of Approval" indicating high quality large print. We are delighted that Thorndike Press is one of the publishers whose titles meet these standards. We are also pleased to recognize the significant contribution Thorndike Press is making in this important and growing field.

Lorraine H. Marchi, L.H.D.
Founder/CEO
NAVH

* Thorndike Press encompasses the following imprints: Thorndike, Wheeler, Walker and Large Pr int Press.

CONTENTS

We are bound on some dare devil operation. . . . If successful in the effort both the Government and the people of the US will be astonished.

A. L. DRAYTON,
CONFEDERATE SAILOR,
JUNE 26, 1863

PREFACE

This narrative was drawn from primary sources and interviews with the participants published in contemporary newspapers, allowing me to re-create the drama based exclusively on the testimony of eyewitnesses. I dismissed all reports of scenes and events in secondary sources that I could not firmly establish as fact from the original record, and there were many such instances. Likewise, I omitted any dialogue I could not confirm from firsthand observers who reported in news stories, in their private journals, or in official war records what was said to them or overhead as the story unfolded.

I owe my ability to tell this tale solely to the on-the-scene participants. I am thankful that these individuals recorded the history they lived and that it was saved for posterity in the National Archives, the Library of Congress, and elsewhere. A more lengthy author's note at the end of the book provides additional details regarding research methods and other important factors that went into writing this narrative.

INTRODUCTION

The American Civil War was the bloodiest conflict in the history of the United States. There were almost as many soldiers killed between 1861 and 1865 as were lost in all others from the Revolutionary War to Vietnam. At its end in May 1865, with the final surrender of the last remaining Confederate forces, approximately 620,000 soldiers on both sides were dead from wounds sustained on the battlefield or from the effects of disease. The Civil War still resonates today, though well more than a century has passed, as do the names of the great battles — Chancellorsville, Fredericksburg, Chickamauga, Gettysburg, Shiloh. The fighting raged from Pennsylvania to the New Mexico Territory, and nearly all of it occurred on land or on rivers, bays, and sounds.

But there was another little-known front, one that played itself out on the vast, empty reaches of the world's oceans. Although the Confederacy lacked the resources to field a mighty navy, its leaders understood that maritime commerce represented the life-blood of the Union, and they quickly took steps to send a handful of men on the lonely, thankless mission to destroy as much of it as possible. Eight oceangoing Confederate commerce raiders, as well as a few of their prizes fitted out for cruising, scuttled, burned, captured, or bonded more than two hundred U.S. merchant vessels. They terrorized the maritime business community.

While few in number, Confederate commerce destroyers harpooned the U.S. Merchant Marine and spurred a decline already in progress to end in the nineteenth-century America's bid for supremacy on the high seas. It was not so much the destruction of shipping and cargoes that led to economic ruin, but the reaction of the merchants and insurance underwriters to the risk involved in maritime commerce while rebel gunboats stalked the shipping lanes of the world for Yankee victims. The rates for insuring vessels and cargoes soared. Merchants diverted business from American to foreign-flagged ships, and shipowners sold off their fleets to foreign companies. After the war, the United

States calculated the financial damage to the overall economy at as much as $9 billion. No small surprise, then, that these raiders were called *pirates* in the North, and in coastal cities were among the most hated of the Confederates.

One of the most infamous of these pirates was a young man named Charles William Read, a second lieutenant in the Confederate Navy. Initially Read showed little promise of greatness, evidence of superior intelligence, or ability to lead, until he was given the opportunity to prove himself on the high seas when he took command of a Yankee vessel captured by the CSS *Florida* in 1863 and fitted out as a Confederate raider. Read then found himself locked in a battle of wits with the most senior man in the Navy Department, a wise old Connecticut Yankee serving his country as Abraham Lincoln's Secretary of the Navy. His name was Gideon Welles. Set against the backdrop of Robert E. Lee's advance toward Gettysburg in the early summer of 1863, these two unlikely adversaries squared off in a whirlwind of dramatic events that shocked the North and caused widespread panic in cities from New York to Portland, Maine. Overshadowed by the horror and bloodshed that occurred at

Gettysburg between July 1 and July 3, the story of this young Confederate raider stands as an all-but-forgotten chapter of the Civil War on the high seas.

Chapter One

DARING COMBAT

Western Mississippi, Yazoo River,
2:00 a.m., July 15, 1862

Acrid smoke drifted lazily skyward from the tall funnel of the Confederate ironclad *Arkansas*, signifying the activity below in the fire room as the coal heavers set to their work with a will at the open doors of the furnaces beneath the boilers. The dull light of a lantern flickered in the pilothouse, but little of it was visible from outside. Only a swath of yellow penetrated the shadows from the port cut into the iron to give the commander and the two river pilots a view ahead without being exposed to enemy fire.

Arkansas was a cumbersome vessel, ugly to the seaman accustomed to the sharp lines of a full-rigged sailing ship. Her main deck hardly cleared the water's surface, and the oak-and-iron–reinforced walls protecting the guns resembled a boxlike fort. In the darkness on the water below the diminutive heights of Haynes Bluff, her form loomed above the landing — indistinct, like a small island merged with the shore.

The spring rains had come and gone, and with the onset of summer the water level of the river began to drop. Drawing fourteen feet, *Arkansas* was deep for work on a tributary of the Mississippi River. On each bank of the Yazoo rose a dense forest choked with briars and vines, and blowdown was piled high from the endless cycle of passing thunderstorms and annual inundation that temporarily spread an inland sea across the Mississippi flood plain. Overhanging branches might easily snag the smokestack, or one of the many shoals might easily trap the ironclad, making her a prize of any patrols sent from the two Union fleets anchored several hours away just above Vicksburg beyond DeSoto Point on the Mississippi River.

The nearly two hundred men down below, deep inside the ironclad, prepared for the battle to come as the ship's deckhands cast off the lines and the pilots muttered commands to the helmsman, who turned the wheel as directed. Orders were relayed via a tin speaking tube to the engineers on duty at the ship's two low-pressure steam engines. The 165-foot warship maneuvered away from the shore into midchannel, and started slowly downriver keeping just enough way on to maintain steerage in the current. Men moved about on the gundeck filling the tubs between the guns with fresh water for the sponges needed to swab the barrels after each shot, lest a lingering spark prematurely explode the next charge rammed home.

Other crewmen poured sand around the guns to soak up blood and help prevent the gunners and powder boys from slipping. They piled bandages and tourniquets at various locations while the surgeons below on the berth deck readied the surgery. The instruments, forceps, and saws — shone brightly in the dim light. Down below, the churn of the ship's twin propellers was a dull roar.

In the aft section of the gundeck, Second Lieutenant Charles W. Read supervised the loading of the two six-inch stern rifles capable of firing exploding shells deadly to any wooden ship they might hit. The two gun crews under his command rammed home cartridge bags filled with powder, and followed them with wads and shells. When this was done, the gun captains plunged sharp metal picks down the vent holes at the breeches of the cannons to break open the powder bags. Primers and lanyards were made ready, and the guns were run out. The still air smelled of the river, dank and primal, of mud and ooze, and the heavy odor of the closely packed men, their sweat in the humid night darkening their uniforms and dampening their brows.

Standing near one of his guns, Read satisfied himself that his battery was ready for action, then leaned on the cannon and gazed out the gunport. He well understood what would come with the dawn — the thrill and rush of war, the cries of the wounded, and the possibility that he might not live to see another day. He was already battle-hardened from bloody engagements on the upper and lower Mississippi River, and had learned under fire what he failed to at the U.S. Naval Academy in Annapolis. By all accounts of those who knew him, he was unafraid to fight. Rather than fearing war, he liked the excitement.

Read was a short man of slight build with a sharp, angular face adorned with a slender brown mustache and a goatee. A native of Satartia, Mississippi, a small town about twenty miles downriver from Yazoo

City, he was soft-spoken and often taciturn, even when on liberty in the company of his fellow lieutenants, though he was fiercely loyal to his few friends. Like so many officers in the Confederate Navy, he resigned his commission in the Union Navy during the spring of 1861. His brief stint in the U.S. Navy, most of which he spent as a midshipman aboard the steam cruiser *Powhatan*, stationed in the Gulf of Mexico, provided him with few opportunities to better himself as an officer or to acquire important skills and knowledge of naval warfare.

Read's lackluster record at the Naval Academy in Annapolis likewise revealed nothing to indicate bright prospects as an officer in charge of ships and men in peacetime or in combat. He had taken his final examinations at Annapolis in June 1860, graduating at the age of twenty, and finishing last in his class of twenty-five cadets. During his liberal arts and military studies at the academy he racked up a prodigious number of demerits for fighting, profanity, failure to pass room inspection, and other infractions. His lack of discipline and his single-minded self-assurance came close to ending his naval career before it began. A classmate of his, Roswell H.

Lamson, a lieutenant serving in the Union Navy, wrote that Read "was not considered very brilliant, but was one of those wiry, energetic fellows who would attempt anything but study."

Read's worst subject was French. No matter how hard he tried, he failed to master the language. The only word he could pronounce correctly was *savez,* a form of the verb "to know." He evidently took to saying it so often his classmates nicknamed him Savez. In fact, his close friends called him Savez throughout his life.

While Read may not have been a prime candidate as a French interpreter, he showed somewhat more promise in gunnery. He finished fourth from the bottom of his class in the theory of naval gunnery, a complex course of study involving voluminous charts, tables, and calculations required to figure accurate range, trajectory, and bearing for a target, the influence of windage, and, of course, a comprehensive overview of the various types of guns and projectiles found on typical warships of the day. However, when it came to actually firing cannons he exhibited a natural flair for the job. Big guns he could understand, and his instructors noticed and encouraged his affinity for them.

Of all the men aboard, Read was the only one with firsthand knowledge of what lay ahead of *Arkansas*. Several days past, under orders from his commander, Read had ridden hard across fifty miles of rugged terrain through the night to reach the stronghold of Vicksburg. Once there, he presented himself to Major General Earl Van Dorn. Read passed on his captain's concerns about the general's insistence that *Arkansas* should leave her easily defended position on the Yazoo to carry out the risky mission of attacking two Union fleets, then steam down the Mississippi and make for Mobile, destroying enemy gunboats along the way. Van Dorn listened to Read, but he did not change his mind. *Arkansas* would attack without delay and sink the enemy vessels gathered above Vicksburg or be blown up in the process. Infantry and cavalry charges against impossible odds were common in the land war, and thus far the Confederates had proven victorious in most such engagements. Van Dorn saw no reason not to apply similar tactics when it came to the ironclad.

In the company of another officer, Read rode up the east bank of the Mississippi above Vicksburg until he came within sight of the Union fleets. The undergrowth of the forest became so thick that he could ride no further. He crept to the river's edge on foot, and with a field glass surveyed the armada he and his shipmates aboard *Arkansas* would soon confront. The seagoing vessels of Admiral David G. Farragut were anchored in a line along Read's side of the river.

Read had fought Farragut's fleet during the battle of New Orleans the previous April, and he nursed a special grudge against one of the vessels, Gunboat Number Six. It was this ship that had fired a broadside into the CSS *McRea*, on which he had served as the executive officer. It was this ship that had killed his commander, Lieutenant Thomas B. Huger, a fair and brave man to whom he was devoted. Read later wrote that Huger was "an agreeable gentleman," adding that he was the sort of leader he wanted to serve under. Read watched patiently for a time, trying to see the telltale signs of smoke rising from the stacks of the wooden sloops of war.

Convinced that Farragut's ships did not have steam up, Read turned his attention to the ironclads and rams of Admiral Charles H. Davis anchored across the river from Farragut's fleet. Plumes of gray-and-black smoke rose from the stacks of most of Davis's ships. The smoke meant these ships had steam up and could get underway as soon as *Arkansas* hove into view. Of the two fleets, the ironclads and rams ranked as the most dangerous. They had fought their way down the Mississippi to destroy Confederate fortifications and capture cities, squeezing the Confederates from the north while Farragut did the same from the South in the Union's concerted effort to control all of the Mississippi and effectively cut the Confederacy in two. Vicksburg represented the last major Confederate fortress, a city with gun emplacements mounted on the heights above the river, and a series of defenses to protect its landward flanks. Read counted more than thirty large warships and support craft. Some of the mortar boats that had shelled forts Jackson and St. Philip, guarding the lower Mississippi before the fall of New Orleans, were also in the area. *Arkansas*'s mission appeared doomed from the start.

The hours passed in tense silence for the dozens of men crowded into the small confines of *Arkansas*'s gundeck, and for the others lined up below ready to pass cartridge bags, shot, and shells from the magazines along the passageways to the upper deck. The pilots worked the ship skillfully downriver, negotiating each twist and turn with care to stay in midchannel and avoid the shallows that made out from the points on the inside of bends. The first faint tinges of daylight cast the open gunports in dark blue. Soon, the men could make out the features along the shoreline as the sun rose and the warship approached the lower Yazoo.

"Daylight found us seven or eight miles above the mouth of the river," Read later wrote in his *Reminiscences of the Confederate States Navy*. "The morning was warm and perfectly calm; the dense volume of black smoke which issued from our funnel, rose high above the trees, and we knew that the enemy would soon be on the lookout for us. Pretty soon we discovered smoke above the trees below, winding along the course of the crooked Yazoo."

Three Union warships steamed fast upriver on a reconnaissance mission. The USS *Carondelet*, an ironclad mounting thirteen guns, was the most powerful. *Tyler*, a side-wheeler with eight guns, and the ram *Queen of the West* supported her. The rebel vessel came into view. The lookouts noted that she looked chocolate, rather than black, due to the patina of rust on her iron plating. The armor reinforcing her timber casemate was nothing more than railroad iron hastily fitted in place, along with boiler plate. She looked like a great brown monster pushing up a bow wave of murky river water.

The distance between the opposing vessels closed. *Tyler*, the leading ship, fired her bow guns. *Carondelet* followed. The deafening impacts of the shells smashing against *Arkansas*'s forward casemate shook the ship and sent shards of iron from her shield whizzing aft. More shot and shells hit, and the iron began to warp and bend. When her guns came to bear, *Arkansas* returned fire. A shell ripped through *Tyler* and exploded in the engine room, spraying the compartment in blood and gore from the dead and wounded. The Union ships turned back toward the Mississippi. They chose a running fight that would bring the rebel ironclad between the massed guns of the two Union fleets, where it was supposed she would be quickly destroyed.

The roar of cannons, the shriek of shells, and the tremendous explosions from each direct hit rumbled through the countryside. The noise of the cannonading could be heard more than ten miles away. Smoke drifted across the water, and created an unnatural fog that seemed to hang in the still air and spread slowly to each bank of the Yazoo. Both Union and Confederate crews took casualties, the men of *Carondelet* receiving the worst of it with approximately thirty killed, wounded, or missing at the close of the engagement. *Queen of the West*, after ineffectual attempts to ram *Arkansas*, steamed away with all speed, though damaged from several well-aimed projectiles.

Read described in vivid detail the destruction of *Carondelet*:

> We had decreased our distance from the iron-clad rapidly, and were only a hundred yards astern, our shot still raking him, when he ceased firing and sheered into the bank; our engines were stopped, and ranging up alongside, with the muzzles of our guns touching him, we poured in a broadside of solid shot, when his colors came down. . . . on we pushed, driving the two fleeing boats ahead of us, our speed decreasing all the time, owing to shot holes in the smoke stack; but in a few minutes the "Arkansas" glided out into the broad Mississippi, right into the midst of the hostile fleet.

In addition to casualties among the crew, *Arkansas* had sustained serious damage. Holes riddled the smokestack, reducing the flow of air available to efficiently fire the boilers. The connection between the funnel and the furnaces had been shot to pieces, and flames from the furnaces heated the gundeck. The temperature inside the ship rose to above 120 degrees, steam pressure decreased, and the ironclad's propellers turned more slowly every minute.

As *Arkansas* emerged from the Yazoo, the engines could hardly keep her moving fast enough to maintain steerage in the swift river current. Her captain, who had been wounded, nevertheless kept to his post. He ordered her turned downriver toward the safety of Vicksburg. In the brief interlude before the next battle, he observed the "forest of masts and smokestacks" and the "panoramic effect . . . intensified by the city of men spread out with innumerable tents opposite on the right bank." The Union fleets were not ready to get underway and the men aboard the ships rushed to bring their guns to bear. One of the first to slip her cable and close in was Gunboat Number Six.

Manning his station at the bow guns, Lieutenant George W. Gift recognized the

29

ship. "The first vessel which stood out to engage us was 'No. 6', against which we had a particular grudge, inspired by Read, who desired us all to handle roughly any sea-going vessel we should see with 'No. 6' on her smoke-stack. . . . I sent my powder boy to Read with a message to come forward, as his friend was in sight."

Although it was risky for a gunnery officer to encourage a peer to leave his post at the start of what promised to be a fierce and bloody naval engagement, Gift indeed sent for Read. Read evidently did not think there was anything wrong in temporarily abandoning his station and went forward to see his "friend." Like two boys in a schoolyard, the lieutenants watched Gunboat Number Six draw near through the gunport. All of *Arkansas*'s officers, except the captain, were inexperienced young men. Though they had passed muster at Annapolis, they were not rooted in the discipline and training of traditional navy standards.

"[Read] came leisurely and carelessly, swinging a primer lanyard, and I think I have never looked at a person displaying such remarkable coolness and self-possession," Gift wrote years later in an article published in the *Southern Historical Society Papers*. "On observing the numbers ahead his eye was as bright and his smile as genuine as if he had been about to join a company of friends instead of enemies."

Read returned to his post at the stern, ever hopeful that Gunboat Number Six would stray into range of his guns. The record does not indicate if Read got his chance for revenge. However, Gift reported:

We were now getting close aboard "No. 6", and he sheered with his port helm and unmuzzled his eleven-inch pivot gun charged with grape. It was hastily pointed, and the charge fell too low to enter our ports, for which it was intended. This broke the terrible quiet which hung over us like a spell. Every man's nerves were strung up again, and we were ready for the second battle. With a sharp touch of the starboard helm Brady [*Arkansas*'s Mississippi River pilot] showed me "No 6" straight ahead, and I gave him a shell through and through, and as we passed he got the port broadside. He did not follow us up. These two shots opened the engagement.

Arkansas steamed slowly between the two lines of ships, running a gauntlet of heavy fire that her captain compared to a

31

"volcano." The pounding of shot and shell was continuous, as was the return fire from the crews at the rebel ironclad's ten guns. Smoke obscured the surface of the river and the vessels as well. It hung in a thickening cloud, and blinded the gunners on both sides. They found their targets by the flashes of cannons. The noise deafened them. Inside *Arkansas*, the men panted for breath in the furnace that was their ship, and coughed and gagged from the smoke of the guns. On she steamed, dodging and disabling rams, ripping apart Farragut's wooden ships, and hotly engaging Davis's ironclads.

The Union fleets closed in, surrounding *Arkansas*. Bits of her armor blew off the casemate and allowed projectiles to breach the ship's shield in the bow section. One shell alone killed sixteen men and wounded many more. Gift described the inside of the casemate as a slaughterhouse. "A great heap of mangled and ghastly slain lay on the gundeck, with rivulets of blood running away from them. There was a poor fellow torn asunder, another mashed flat . . . brains, hair and blood were all about." Read, who was far less descriptive in his recollections, simply said the shells and shot had done "fearful execution amongst our men."

Arkansas's port side weakened. The fasteners holding the iron in place ripped away under the continuous pounding of the Union guns. As the entire ship shuddered, inching her way downriver, the shield of armor threatened to fall to pieces and expose the crew to the full fury of the cannonade. The pilot strained to see ahead. DeSoto Point hove into view. Riding the current, the steam pressure in her boilers almost gone, the ship drew under the protective guns of Vicksburg to the cheers of thousands of jubilant residents gathered on the heights above the river.

The Union fleets attempted to destroy *Arkansas* later that same night and for some days afterward, but with no success. Davis and Farragut abandoned Vicksburg, earning them reproach from Secretary of the Navy Gideon Welles. On August 10, 1862, Welles received word that *Arkansas*'s crew had run her aground and blown her up to keep the ship from falling into Union hands. She had been pinned down on August 6 during a Confederate counteroffensive to retake Baton Rouge, an effort that failed in large part because of the presence of U.S. gunboats firing in support of the hard-pressed army forces fighting at the river's edge. Welles knew that the failure to capture Vicksburg meant the war would be prolonged, and he blamed the army for it. While *Arkansas*'s role in the battle represented more an irritating embarrassment than a decisive factor contributing to the Union's withdrawal, he looked on it as a black mark against both flag officers, and indirectly, on his own reputation as well.

Vicksburg should have been taken by the first of June, but no adequate cooperating military force was furnished, and as a consequence our largest squadron in the Gulf and our flotilla in the Mississippi have been detained and injured. The most disreputable naval affair of the War was the descent of the steam ram Arkansas through both squadrons till she hauled in under the batteries of Vicksburg, and there the two flag officers abandoned the place and the ironclad ram, Farragut and his force going down to New Orleans, and Davis proceeding with his flotilla up the river. I have written them both, briefly but expressively, on the subject of the ram Arkansas. . . .

There were other disreputable naval affairs just over the horizon. On the evening of

September 3, 1862, the Confederate commerce destroyer *Florida* reached the waters off Mobile, Alabama, and the next day ran through the flotilla of Union warships blockading the port. She had only a skeleton crew — men stricken with yellow fever while fitting the raider out with gun batteries transported to Bahamian waters aboard a British-flagged vessel operating on behalf of the Confederacy. When she was safely anchored in the bay, though badly damaged during the transit, her captain, John Newland Maffitt, began organizing men to make repairs.

Maffitt also started his search for young officers to assist him in his future mission. He wanted brave, capable men, sailors whom he could rely on to follow orders and do their duty while facing the uncertainties of a ship that must live on the spoils of her victims, a ship that would be hunted and pursued wherever she went. In his quest for such men, the name of a young Mississippian came to his attention. That man was Charles W. Read, and Maffitt put his influence to work to have him transferred to his command. The decision had far-reaching consequences that Maffitt never could have foreseen, and that Welles would find far more threatening than simply an irritating embarrassment.

Chapter Two

HIGH SEAS TERROR

New York Harbor, October 16, 1862

The brig *Golden Lead* slowly worked her way northward up the Main Ship Channel bound for the crowded anchorage on the flats off Governors Island in the upper bay of New York Harbor. Staten Island and the quarantine station on its waterfront receded astern. The light southerly wind and a fair tide pushed the brig through the Narrows, and the low skyline of the city gradually took shape ahead. The spire of Trinity Church, the tallest landmark on the seaward tip of Manhattan, projected above all the other buildings. It had been an eventful passage from the Isle of Jersey across a sea crowded with more than peaceful merchantmen engaged in the routine transportation of goods and passengers to distant ports. The master of the brig stood on the poop deck beside the pilot guiding the vessel safely through the shoals above the Sandy Hook bar, and looked with sympathy upon the eight men who had been strangers just ten days since.

The men gathered together on the lee-ward side of the poop deck, out of defer-ence to the master, and each stared at the city. No doubt they wondered what their prospects might be now that they had lost their ships to the enemy. Three were cap-tains, and one — George Hagar of the ship *Brilliant* — had lost everything he owned. He unwisely thought the seas were safe enough to sail without paying for war risk insurance. The rates had soared after the start of the rebellion, and Hagar, like many shipowners and masters, could not afford it. A growing number of American ships stayed in port or were sold to businessmen in neutral countries. Times were bad for the U.S. Merchant Marine. It did not appear that they would improve in the foreseeable future.

When *Golden Lead* reached the flats, her officers and crew brought her head to the wind and current. The headsails luffed in the gentle breeze. With her topsails backed, the vessel lost way. Her bow began to pay off as the anchor, freed from the cathead, plunged into the shallow water, the chain rattling and sparking against the iron rim of the hawshole. Her bow came again to face south, her sprit and jibboom pointing straight down the bay at the Narrows. Topmen aloft furled her square sails, while deckhands set to coiling the lines neatly on the pins at the rails and the bases of the masts. It was a familiar bit of work to all aboard. However, for the eight passengers, the routine activity of the crew inspired memories of their unlucky encounters with the Confederate raider *Alabama*.

In the fall of 1862, the Confederacy's plans to field commerce destroyers to cripple the Union's maritime enterprise resulted in the completion and deployment of two swift, modern vessels, *Florida* and *Alabama*. Early in the war, the Confederate government realized it would have to rely on Britain and, to a lesser extent, France for the building and arming of warships. The South's lack of skilled labor and shipyards capable of constructing ships suitable for combat on the high seas required the Confederates to seek foreign assistance. Before this was possible, they needed to work around existing British statutes and laws that technically forbade active cooperation in support of the war effort.

On May 13, 1861, Britain issued a

Proclamation of Neutrality. By recognizing the Confederacy as a belligerent power, it greatly favored the South, according it the same rights and restrictions as the United States in dealings with Great Britain, such as terms upon which a vessel from either side might enter British ports, obtain supplies, and make repairs. This was just short of recognition as an independent nation for legal and political purposes. Under international law, a blockade was meant as a recourse against a foreign enemy, so Lincoln's blockade effectively legitimized Britain's quasirecognition of the Confederacy. Had Lincoln merely closed the ports, the South would not have received the advantages of a belligerent power. On the other hand, the United States would not then have been legally able to seize neutral ships bound for blockaded ports and otherwise efficiently choke off maritime trade with the Confederacy.

However advantageous the rights of a belligerent may have been, the proclamation's prohibition against the sale of warships was a problem for the South. The stipulations of the Foreign Enlistment Act of 1819 also prohibited British subjects without official sanction to build or arm warships for a belligerent power. There were no limits, though, on the sale of weapons, ammunition, uniforms, or provisions to either side, and there were no limits on building vessels provided that they were not armed. With the help of British attorneys, Confederate agents took advantage of the numerous loopholes in the Proclamation of Neutrality and the Foreign Enlistment Act. British entrepreneurs saw a great opportunity to earn substantial profits from the American Civil War, and were only too happy to cooperate with representatives of the Confederacy. They also profited from sending goods through the blockade.

British foreign policy made it easy for the Confederates to get what they wanted and to operate freely in English ports. The nation stood to gain much if the Union split apart and the United States lost its clout as an emerging world power. Cotton from the South would continue to flow into Britain's major manufacturing centers, and America's merchant marine, second only in size and importance in global economics to England, would no longer be able to compete as it once did. It was a natural inclination, however reprehensible it may have been from the American point of view, given the jockeying for power that had taken place in a bloodless manner between Britain and the United States since the close of the War of 1812. Neither Britain nor France wanted to get directly involved in the American conflict, but each stood to profit through indirect involvement. Each commenced a careful dance around international laws toward that end.

Acting under orders from the Confederate government to build and equip commerce raiders, former U.S. naval officer James Dunwoody Bulloch crossed the Atlantic and reached Liverpool on June 4, 1861. He was authorized to spend more than a half-million dollars on the two ships that were to become *Florida* and *Alabama*. To avoid any chance of diplomatic complications, Bulloch arranged it so that the ships were, on paper, not intended for the Confederacy but rather for third parties. Title would change hands once the ships were at sea and clear of British waters. Both British and United States officials knew full well what Bulloch was doing. Yet, the vessels did not appear to be property of the Confederacy and were apparently being built for peaceful service as merchantmen. Construction was allowed to proceed. Bulloch instructed the shipyards not to arm the raiders, but instead purchased the guns and other equipment he needed separately and exported the war materiel from England on British transports.

Thus, William C. Miller & Sons of Liverpool went to work on a ship called *Oreto*, and during the course of 1861, she took shape on the ways at the edge of the Mersey River. She was a vessel of 700 tons displacement, 191 feet on deck, and two steam engines of 200 horsepower each turned a single propeller. The design was similar to that of an English gunboat, and her three masts raked aft gave her the sleek look of a topsail schooner meant for the racecourse. She sailed from Liverpool in March of 1862 and was rechristened CSS *Florida* en route to Mobile, Alabama on August 17, 1862.

As laborers secured *Oreto*'s frames to her keelson, then set to plank her hull, men across the river were busy at Birkenhead Iron Works on hull 290. Slightly larger than *Oreto*, 290 displaced approximately nine hundred tons and extended 230 feet on deck. Her engine developed 300 horsepower and also drove a single screw. Barkentine-rigged, she would cruise better off the wind than *Oreto*, but both ships were able to maintain an average speed of ten knots under most conditions. Both ships were equipped with mechanisms to raise the propeller into wells built in the under-bodies of the hulls — an innovative feature to reduce drag under sail. An expert in merchant and naval shipping, Bulloch knew good craftsmanship when he saw it. He was well pleased with the work of these shipyards. After fitting out in the Azores, hull 290 was christened CSS *Alabama* on August 24, 1862. She made her first capture on September 5, under the command of veteran U.S. naval officer Raphael Semmes, former master of an earlier Confederate raider, CSS *Sumter*, which had been laid up and later sold in Gibraltar.

Along with others involved in the scheme to send vessels of the Confederate Navy after peaceful Union ships, Bulloch did not fail to see the immorality of the practice. War was meant to embroil opposing combat forces, not civilians or their property. Total war was a novel concept, one that did not sit well with gentlemen warriors. The conflict changed the conduct of war, introducing advanced technologies in weapons that made the old ways of fighting obsolete. Infantry charges against fortified positions behind earthworks and trenches cost tens of thousands of lives in a single engagement. The field of battle spread to encompass the land and its people. The struggle already had caused the destruction of homes and businesses, and the death of innocents on both sides. If noncombatants at sea suffered because of the raiders, that was a sad, though acceptable, reality of the rebellion. Bulloch wrote:

> There can be no doubt that the destruction of unarmed and peaceful merchant ships, while quietly pursuing their voyages on the high seas, is a practice not defensible upon the principles of the moral law. . . . [But] when two nations unhappily fall out and go to war, the government of each does its best to inflict the greatest possible amount of injury upon the other on the principle that the more burdensome and afflicting the state of war can be made to the opposing party, the more quickly will he consent to terms of peace.

Maffitt described the mission and the intended results of the commerce destroyers in his private journal: "When a man-of-war is sacrificed, 'tis a national calamity, not individually felt; but when merchant ships are destroyed upon the high seas individuality suffers, and the shoe then pinches in the right direction. All the merchants of New York and Boston, who have by their splendid traders become princes in wealth, and puffy with patriotic zeal for the subjugation of the South, will soon cry, 'peace, peace.' " Maffitt was correct. The actions of the raiders did indeed cause many in wealthy circles to put pressure on the Lincoln administration to do its utmost to end the war as quickly as possible, and the news of the depredations of *Alabama* in October was just the beginning.

As the men aboard *Golden Lead* filed ashore in New York City on that autumn day in October 1862, CSS *Alabama* headed steadily westward toward the mainland of the United States. Her captain, Raphael Semmes, harbored a deep-seated desire to sail through the Narrows to fire on the ships in the upper bay and on the city itself. It was an almost suicidal mission to contemplate, for the defenses of New York were strong; but if it succeeded, the blow to Yankee morale would be worth the possible loss of his ship and his men. Only a lack of coal forced Semmes to break off his attacks on transatlantic shipping, the last of which occurred just three hundred miles east of Atlantic City, New Jersey. He sailed southward to carry out even more destruction after resupplying in Venezuela. The people of New York learned of his most recent depredations from Captain Hagar and the others with him, though not of his intentions to attack them on their own soil.

As soon as Captain Hagar and his companions reached the piers of lower Manhattan, the reporters gathered around to hear their tale. The newsmen frequently sought out newly arrived ships, especially those from Britain or France. They were not disappointed with the tidings they received from *Golden Lead*, and the men she had taken aboard in midocean on October 6 after hailing the ship *Emily Farnham* of New Brunswick, Canada, bound from New York to Liverpool with a cargo for British merchants. Prisoners from destroyed American vessels, transferred from *Alabama*, crowded *Emily Farnham*, which was spared because she was a Canadian ship and carried a British-owned cargo. Her water and food were in short supply, and the master of *Golden Lead* agreed to take eight prisoners. After the transfer, he went on his way with doubled lookouts and all sail set for New York.

The reporters finished their interviews and scurried off to their offices to file their stories. The following day, readers of the *New York Herald* opened the paper to the bold headline: A PIRATE ON THE HIGH SEAS: THE DEPREDATIONS OF THE REBEL CRUISER ALABAMA, BETTER KNOWN AS "NO. 290." Columns of text comprised mostly of testimony from the late prisoners filled the pages, and provided a glimpse of what it was like to endure capture at the hands of the rebels. Prior to the transfer of prisoners to *Emily Farnham*, more than one hundred men were chained in irons on *Alabama*'s main deck. Exposed to wind, rain, and the seas that washed through the open gunports, the men suffered terribly.

According to Captain S. R. Tilton, master of the whaling bark *Virginia*, of New Bedford, which was captured and burned on September 17, "The steamer's guns being kept run out, the side ports could not be shut; and when the seas was a little rough, or the vessel rolled, the water was continually coming in on both sides, and swashing across the deck where we were, so that our feet and clothing were wet all the time, either from the water below or the rain above. We were obliged to sleep in the place where we were, and often waked up in the night nearly under water. . . . We were kept on deck all the time, night and day, and a guard placed over us."

The story also provided details on Semmes as Hagar perceived him. Summarizing the captain, the reporter for the *Herald* gave the following description of the rebel commander:

[Semmes] sports a huge mustache . . . and it is evident that it occupies much of his attention. His steward waxes it every day carefully, and so prominent is it that the sailors of the Alabama term him "Old Beeswax." His whole appearance is that of a corsair, and the transformation appears to be complete from Commander "Raphael Semmes," United States Navy, to a combination of Lafitte, Kidd and Gibbs, the three most notorious pirates the world has ever known.

The news of *Alabama*'s attacks rippled through New York's business district and initially inspired gloom among shipowners, merchants, and insurance underwriters. The financial losses exceeded $1 million for the fourteen ships destroyed since

September 5. Those directly affected were furious about these outrages committed on the high seas. Knowing full well that they might be next, their colleagues fumed too. Not all the ire was directed at the pirate. The fallout hit the U.S. Navy and Gideon Welles.

Wealthy entrepreneurs through the New York Chamber of Commerce, and on their own, petitioned the mayor of New York City, then the state governor, to pressure the secretary of the navy to expand convoys for U.S.-flagged vessels beyond those already guarding ships laden with California gold and U.S. mail from the West Coast. Their counterparts in Boston did the same. While Navy officers and sailors grew rich on prizes captured in attempts to run the blockade, the merchants grew poorer because of the Confederate raiders. In northern cities on the coast, people of means cried for action. What was the Navy for if not to protect the vital economic interests of the United States? When would the destruction end?

Welles, however, remained convinced that a couple of wayward Confederate cruisers constituted far less a threat to the nation than the blockade runners resupplying the enemy, and he was disinclined to draw off resources needed to stop them. The British were the chief offenders. They built and deployed fast ships with shallow drafts to dart across shoals inside the squadrons he had worked assiduously to put in place. Other vessels were converted for use in blockade running — from steamers to schooners — and some had retired British naval officers as captains, who plied their trade under assumed names to avoid the provisions of Britain's Foreign Enlistment Act. In many cases, Southern shipowners transferred registry of their vessels to British merchants to gain the advantages accorded to neutrals. Profits from one voyage often paid the entire building costs of a ship used to run the blockade.

Lincoln had declared a blockade on Confederate ports from South Carolina to Texas on April 19, 1861. On April 27, he extended it to cover Virginia and North Carolina as well. This effectively required Welles to bottle up ports along more than 3,500 miles of coastline laced with navigable inlets, rivers, and well-defended natural harbors. When Welles took over the administration of the Navy Department in March 1861, the U.S. Navy numbered approximately ninety vessels. Only forty-two were in active commission, and less than a dozen cruised in home waters. Establishing and enforcing the blockade was Welles's main objective in those first days of the war, and it was no easy task.

With the help of his assistant, Gustavus Vasa Fox, Welles orchestrated the construction, charter, and purchase of ships as fast as possible. By the end of 1862, he had deployed more than 250 ships for blockade duty and ballooned the prewar roster of 7,500 enlisted men to more than 22,000. He was seeing results by the autumn of 1862. A close look at the numbers revealed that in late December 1861, nine out of ten blockade runners made it through the squadrons he had deployed to stop them. Now, with the large expansion of the Navy well under way, that number had dropped to seven out of eight.

Nevertheless, every time a runner made port loaded with guns and ammunition, it rankled him. It redoubled his determination to plug the leaks and it fanned a deep-seated, though well-controlled, rage at the British, who played such a pivotal role in thwarting his mission. He knew all too well that those cargoes of arms would ultimately cost lives on the battlefield and prolong the war. Although the increased danger to vessels running the blockade represented progress, it was not good enough for Welles. Drawing off any ships from blockade duty would undermine his key mission. However, he was always mindful of political implications, and he was indeed under pressure from the merchants and government officials in New York and Boston. He found himself forced into the position of sending additional ships out for duty on the high seas, for he had already dispatched cruisers in search of privateers and warships of the Confederate Navy engaged in "piratical activities."

He noted in his diary on September 4, 1862: "We hear that our new steamer, the Adirondack, is wrecked. She had been sent to watch the Bahama Channel. Her loss, the discharge of the Oreto by the courts of Nassau [*Oreto*, also known as *Florida*, had been detained in Nassau because of alleged violations of the Foreign Enlistment Act, but was then released], and the arrival of Steamer 290, both piratical British wolves, demand attention, although we have no vessels to spare from the blockade. Must organize a flying squadron, as has been suggested. . . ."

The squadron of swift warships was dispatched, but to the Caribbean, where it was thought the rebel commerce destroyers might be operating. However, no Confederate raiders were currently active there. It was just one of many times that the "wolves" got the best of Gideon Welles, but he was to have his day. All he had to do was be patient, let the corsairs make fatal mistakes, and have his forces ready to strike when they did.

Chapter Three

DARK TIMES

Washington, D.C., January 1, 1863

The sentinels posted at the Navy Yard Bridge spanning the Anacostia River, a tributary of the Potomac, pulled their overcoats snug to ward off the early morning chill, grateful for whatever warmth the winter sun might give. Sunlight sparkled on the water east of the bridge, and a gentle breeze darkened the surface with cats'-paws that temporarily obliterated the deep blue reflected from the clear sky above. The smell of wood smoke filled the air as it rose in gray-white clouds all along the city's defenses — the gun emplacements, forts, and trenches that encircled Washington for thirty-seven miles from its outer heights to the river shores. Like the men guarding the bridge leading to the Navy Yard, other sentinels stood watch at every strategic point.

Behind the defensive perimeter sprawled

the rural, half-finished city, more a back-water than anything else, and with no significant economic importance to the nation. It was not a busy seaport like Boston or New York, nor was it a center of manufacturing. Yet, it was the seat of the government and that imparted great value as a symbol of the Union, however disheveled and incomplete. The obelisk that was to become the Washington Monument remained a mere stub and had been so for years since construction stopped in 1855 for lack of private contributions needed to fund the project. Due east, past the half-developed park of the Mall and the landscaped grounds of the Smithsonian Institution, one of the few attractions in Washington travelers of the day considered well worth a visit, the Capitol's new cast-iron dome was a work in progress. Scaffolds enveloped its ribs and a large crane rose skyward. On each side of the central building, the new wings were not quite done after nearly a decade of labor, though the legislators had moved in.

In total, there were six major public buildings of note in the city — the executive mansion, Capitol, patent office, general post office, Smithsonian Institution, and treasury, and some of these were converted to housing for the wounded, who had turned Washington into an immense hospital. More than one thousand cots lined the corridors of the patent office, and approximately two thousand more were crammed into the Capitol. Wounded filled schools, private homes, and newly built hospitals. After each battle fought within reasonable transport distance to Washington, more men of the Army of the Potomac came in on wagons or on foot, and there was little room for them.

The previous June, the city's churches were one by one given over to the surgeons, nurses, and volunteer wound dressers. Carpenters built raised floors over the pews. Under these floors were spaces packed with boxes of Bibles and hymnbooks, carpets and cushions, furniture and pulpits. Above on the wide squares of open floors were rows of tables covered with rubber mats, and the ubiquitous cots for the men waiting for or recovering from their operations. Church bells could not be rung in celebration of the Fourth of July in 1862. The bases of the bell towers were packed with the dead and dying. And still they came. As the shadows diminished and the city stirred awake to greet the new year, many of the recent casualties from Fredericksburg crowded the wards.

Such were the realities of Washington and the nation on the first day of 1863. Few dared hope that the war might soon end, as so many had when the conflict began in April 1861. The people of the North looked to Washington for answers, for some solution to find a way to peace while preserving the Union. Upon the shoulders of a handful of leaders rested the lives of the multitude, and the responsibility constituted a heavy burden. It did not allow for the interference of personal wants and needs, nor for personal tragedies. For Gideon Welles, the times were indeed dark, filled with a sense of calamity that spread over him like the coming of night.

On New Year's Day, Welles awoke later than usual and prepared for his obligatory visit to the executive mansion at 11:00 a.m. After the servants cleared away the breakfast dishes, Welles, a large, corpulent man of sixty, whose rather unconvincing wig and long, white beard earned him the moniker of Father Neptune, shrugged on a heavy overcoat and turned to his wife, Mary. In mourning for their three-year-old son, Hubert, who had died suddenly from diphtheria just six weeks ago, Mary was dressed completely in black. They had been married for twenty-seven years and she had given birth to nine children. Only three of them, all sons, still lived. Welles took his leave, saying he would not be long at the official gathering of Army and Navy officers in audience before the president at the executive mansion, an annual rite that marked the start of each new year and preceded the public reception scheduled to begin at noon.

It was easier for Welles than his wife to bear up under the grief. Their sadness was a palpable presence in the house. Now, more than ever, he buried himself in his work. He did so in part out of necessity, for the war was not going well, but also because in his duty he found distraction. Fatigue he almost welcomed. His exhaustion tempered his inclination to stay up late at night, the house dark except for his lamp in the study, Mary asleep in their bedroom. In those quiet hours, he leaned back in his chair with the clay pipe he enjoyed smoking and silently grieved for Hubert, the sound from the pendulum of the nearby clock beating like a steady heart.

Welles had sent Mary, Hubert, and another son, John, to stay with a friend on the Hudson River until the first frost came to Washington in November. It was a common practice. Most people of means left the city because of the increased incidence of disease that occurred in the hot, humid summer. They returned when it was thought safe, after the first freeze, and the schedule of receptions and parties filled out and lasted till spring. Having lost five of his children — two daughters and three sons — to typhoid and other illnesses, he had insisted Mary take Hubert away to New York. In spite of his caution, yet another child lay dead at Spring Grove Cemetery in Hartford, Connecticut. The continuation of a long series of personal tragedies weighed heavily upon him. To his diary he confided, "Well has it been for me that overwhelming public duties have borne down upon me in these sad days. Alas, frail life! amid the nation's grief I have my own. . . ."

Welles left the house at around 10:30 a.m. and walked briskly toward the wide expanse of Lafayette Square, a rectangular park fronting the north side of the White House, which he could see from his front stoop. Although not in direct view, just to the west of the executive mansion were the modest residences that housed the war and navy departments. All were within an easy walk from the estate he had leased for four years at the princely sum of $1,500 per annum.

A man of established means from an inheritance left him by his father, as well as a number of solid investments, Welles was used to living an upper-class lifestyle. However, in past years his fortune had declined. Since coming to Washington, he had found that the expense of keeping up a standard of living commensurate with his rank as a member of Lincoln's cabinet took most of his annual salary of $8,000, leaving little or nothing to save and invest. He was not in Washington to get rich, but to serve his country. Political and economic realities represented a transitory existence as unpredictable as life itself, and he resigned himself to such uncertainties.

Over his long career in politics, first as a Democrat, then as a Republican, Welles consistently held liberal, progressive views on law and government, and he exercised them in his early days in the Connecticut legislature, to which he was elected at the age of twenty-four. Between 1827 and 1835, he lobbied to reform the laws of the state to abolish imprisonment of individuals simply because they were indebted to creditors, to moderate strict religious tests before a person could bear witness in a court of law, and to ease restrictions mandating that male citizens of Connecticut must own property and adhere to specific religious requirements in order to vote. In his subsequent positions — state comptroller of public accounts, postmaster of Hartford, chief of the Bureau of Provisions and Clothing for the U.S. Navy, and others — he was a devoted adherent of the values favoring the power of an individual to pursue in freedom whatever might be possible in an egalitarian society, and the right of the states to chart their own course within the larger fabric of the Union.

As times changed and the Democratic party to which he was faithful became increasingly the party of slavery, disillusionment grew in Welles. He did not support slavery and considered it immoral for many of the same reasons the abolitionists did. It was wrong to own human beings, and he also thought it contradicted the basic philosophy of the United States. That a nation could stand for freedom and yet support slavery struck him as a sad paradox. This led to a radical move based solely on his personal convictions and his courage to stand behind them. It was a change that ultimately landed him his current position even though he was a land-lubber at heart, and had never commanded a sailing ship in the clutches of a gale or in the fire of battle.

Against strong antislavery opposition, the Democratic-controlled Congress in May 1854 passed the Kansas-Nebraska Act, which, in essence, proved a major victory for supporters of slavery by permitting it in these two new territories if the people living there voted in favor of the institution. Welles was one of the key players in organizing lobby efforts against the bill. When it was enacted, he quit the Democratic party in disgust. He helped organize the fledgling Republican party later that same year, and had been influential in it ever since in his positions as a Republican national committeeman and a member of the national executive committee. He was also chairman of Connecticut's delegation at the Chicago convention, which nominated Abraham Lincoln as its candidate for president.

Welles made his way across Lafayette Square to the east wing of the executive mansion, and arrived before 11:00 a.m. Members of the cabinet were already there, gathered around President Lincoln.

The president had been up early to put the last touches on his final version of the Emancipation Proclamation. Though he looked tired, he nevertheless smiled at his advisers and carried on his characteristically good-tempered banter. He was an imposing presence. Walt Whitman, who was in Washington in early 1863 as a volunteer helping to tend the wounded, described him with his typical flair for language: "He has a face like a Hoosier Michael Angelo, so awful ugly it becomes beautiful, with its strange mouth, its deep cut, crisscross lines, and its doughnut complexion."

Just minutes earlier, Lincoln had signed the Emancipation Proclamation, freeing the slaves in all regions then in active rebellion against the United States. Issued in preliminary form on September 22, 1862, the Emancipation Proclamation was a highly controversial document outlining an equally controversial policy. Some, including Welles, thought it unconstitutional, a measure that exceeded the power of the executive branch of government. Others thought it was unfair because it did not free slaves in states loyal to the Union and in portions of Confederate territory under Union control out of fear that such action would divide the North and cause states on the borders of the Confederacy to secede. Slaves in bondage in the South were the supposed target of the proclamation, but it certainly would not lead to their immediate freedom, and as such it seemed something of a paper tiger.

Lincoln was well aware of this, and the apparent injustice of the outcome for the slaves in Union states who would not be freed. Yet, it was necessary from his viewpoint to protect the greater good of the United States. He gambled that the proclamation in preliminary form might cause rebel states to return to the Union. In effect, the policy approved the continuation of slavery in any state that rejoined the Union, a paradox not lost on Lincoln. Since slavery was so important to the cotton-based economy of the South, he used it as a carrot, an incentive to bring the rebel states back into the fold, with slavery intact. It was a tradeoff and he knew it. Although he hated slavery, Lincoln's main intent was to sew the torn fabric of American society back together any way he could.

The proclamation failed to achieve the desired outcome. Rather than drive Confederate states back into the Union, it bolstered the South's conviction to win independence. Thus, when the proclamation went into effect officially, on January 1, 1863, it represented very little in real terms at the time. The status quo remained, and if anything, the situation was far worse given the added resolve of the Confederacy to break away from the Union.

One happy result, however, was that a slave who managed to escape from a Confederate state would be free if he or she made it to Union-held territory. Tens of thousands of slaves made their way to the North and joined the war effort; they were especially welcome in the Navy, which had been open to black sailors even before the war. On July 22, 1861, well ahead of the Army, which began enlisting black soldiers after January 1, 1863, Welles issued orders to his senior naval officers to offer shelter and protection to slaves able to cross into Union territory. On September 25, three days after the initial release of the Emancipation Proclamation, he ordered his officers to enlist any former slave who wished to join the Navy. The Navy desperately needed sailors to man the rapidly expanding fleet, and Welles saw no reason to deny a former slave the chance to fight against his former master. Black sailors took on a wide variety of duties aboard ship and contributed much to the success of the Navy. By the war's end, one out of four men serving on U.S. Navy ships was black.

Welles was one of the first of Lincoln's advisers to learn of the president's intentions regarding the Emancipation Proclamation back in July 1862. He considered the policy with ambivalence. He was one of the people close to the president to state his deep reservations about Lincoln's authority to take such "despotic" measures. Welles saw the policy as despotic because it treaded on states' rights, the preservation of which the South used as part of the reasoning for seeking independence in the first place. It seemed to lend credence to the Confederate point of view that the federal government was interfering in state matters it had no business meddling with. Because of this, politicians and businessmen across a wide spectrum entertained reservations about whether the proclamation was a good idea.

Welles also doubted that the policy would accomplish the main objective of getting the South to rejoin the Union. As he exchanged congratulations with the president on New Year's Day, he still questioned the wisdom of the measure. However, he generally approved of it in view of developments during the previous autumn. In September, he wrote:

For myself the subject has, from its magnitude and its consequences, oppressed me, aside from the ethical features of the question. It is a step in the progress of this war which will extend into the distant future. A favorable termination of this terrible conflict seems more remote with every movement, and unless the Rebels hasten to avail themselves of the alternative presented, of which I see little probability, the war can scarcely be other than one of emancipation to the slave, or subjugation, or submission to their Rebel owners.

There is in the Free States a very general impression that this measure will insure a speedy peace. I cannot say that I so view it. No one in those States dare advocate peace as a means of prolonging slavery, even if it is his honest opinion, and the pecuniary, industrial, and social sacrifice impending will intensify the struggle before us. While, however, these dark clouds are above and around us, I cannot see how the subject can be avoided. Perhaps it is not desirable it should be. It is, however, an arbitrary and despotic measure in the cause of freedom.

As he stood talking with the other members of Lincoln's cabinet, Welles was merely going through the motions of the ceremonial event, putting in his mandatory time before he was free to return home. Soon, the diplomatic corps began to arrive. The Emancipation Proclamation was the key subject of discussion. Almost everyone realized the importance of the occasion; in the formal adoption of the policy, the character of the war had suddenly taken on a more noble impetus. It was no longer a fight to preserve the Union, but a struggle to obliterate the evil of slavery, the basis for the conflict.

In his position as Secretary of the Navy, Welles was constantly involved in matters of foreign affairs, most particularly the tense and often bellicose relations between Great Britain and the United States. He realized that Lincoln's proclamation might tilt British public opinion more in favor of the United States than it had previously. Yet, he was wise enough to understand that the underlying and, he believed, malicious motives the British had in their support of the rebels would not disappear with the introduction of a publicly stated policy to abolish slavery in the South. From the very outset of the rebellion the British had facilitated the Confederacy's efforts to run the blockade, providing safe harbor for their ships and failing to aggressively enforce the stipulations of the Proclamation of Neutrality and the Foreign Enlistment Act. While Secretary of State Seward tended to placate them, Welles took a much firmer view, which brought him in conflict with Seward on a nearly continual basis.

We are insulted, wronged, and badly treated by the British authorities, especially at Nassau, and I have called the attention of the Secretary of State repeatedly to the facts, but he fears to meet them. After degrading ourselves, we shall be compelled to meet them. I am for no rash means, but I am clearly and decidedly for maintaining our rights. Almost all the aid which the Rebels have received in arms, munitions, and articles contraband have gone to them through the professedly neutral British port of Nassau. From them the Rebels have derived constant encouragement and support, from the commencement of hostilities. Our officers and people are treated with superciliousness and contempt by the authorities and inhabitants, and scarcely a favor or courtesy is extended to them while they are showered upon the Rebels. It is there that vessels are prepared to run the blockade and violate our laws, by the connivance and with the knowledge of the Colonial, and, I apprehend, the parent, government.

The news of British-built cruisers set loose on the shipping of the United States under a rebel flag proved even more vexing to Welles. It represented direct involvement on the part of the British in swaying events in favor of the Confederacy at the expense of Union blood and treasure. On *Alabama*'s attacks the previous autumn and his perception of British complicity in making them possible, he wrote in his diary on October 18: "The ravages by the roving steamer 290, alias Alabama, are enormous. England should be held accountable for these outrages. The vessel was built in England and has never been in the ports of any other nation. British authorities were warned of her true character repeatedly before she left."

Welles did not confine his displeasure to the British. He frequently found himself at odds against the old traditions of the U.S. Navy with regard to the accepted standards by which an officer was promoted. Just because an officer held a senior rank did not mean he was the best man for a given assignment. Welles disregarded whenever possible any political pressure exerted to influence him to hand over an important job to individuals based solely on position and connections. He often promoted junior officers over their more senior counterparts, and this bred resentment in those passed over for distinguished commands. He also brooked few lapses in the men he entrusted.

One unlucky man who failed to carry out his duty to Welles's standards was George Preble. On September 4, 1862, while serving as captain of the sloop *Oneida* on blockade duty off Mobile Bay with the gunboat *Winona* also under his command, Preble observed a sleek-looking vessel approaching at speed. She flew the British flag, and based on her build, appeared to be an English ship. He hesitated before taking aggressive action to stop her and realized too late that she was the rebel gunboat then commonly known as *Oreto* attempting to pass through the blockade. Despite a sustained and heavy fire during a chase lasting more than two hours, *Oreto* reached safe harbor.

"Preble, by sheer pusillanimous neglect, feebleness, and indecision, let the pirate steamer *Oreto* run the blockade," Welles wrote upon receiving the news. "She came right up and passed him, flying English colors. Instead of checking her advance or sinking her, he fired all round, made a noise, and is said to have hurt none of her English crew. This case must be investigated and an example made." Taking the case directly to Lincoln to avoid any possibility that Preble's dereliction of duty, at least in Welles's view, be excused were the matter brought before a board of inquiry or adjudicated in a general court-martial, Welles recommended that the president dismiss him by executive order.

"Dismiss him," Lincoln said. "If that is your opinion, it is mine. I will do it."

When *Florida*'s exploit got out, Welles faced a barrage of barbs and insults from the press on both sides of the Atlantic. He was blamed for the shortcomings of his officers. Some suggested he was not capable of administering the Navy, that he was a befuddled old man playing out of his league. *Punch,* the sardonic British magazine, frequently published witty little poems. The editors came up with a special one for Welles. It read in part:

There was an old fogy named Welles,
Quite worthy of cap and bells,
For he tho't that a pirate,
Who steamed at a great rate,
Would wait to be riddled with shells.

Thus, Welles was keenly aware as he shook the hands of British diplomats on New Year's Day that the ongoing tensions between Britain and the United States would not likely ease because of Lincoln's proclamation concerning the issue of slavery in the South. He was too wise for that. Public opinion in Britain might make it more difficult for a direct intervention in favor of the Confederacy, but the profits for British businessmen and the advantages to Britain that would result from a greatly weakened United States in terms of global power and prestige meant a continuation of the status quo. A great Union victory was needed, a battle that might at last cripple the South's ability to make war and show all the world that the United States was not about to surrender its glory.

Just when that day might come, Welles did not know. After presenting his most senior officers to Lincoln at 11:30 a.m., Welles left the president and his colleagues in the cabinet before noon. He walked past the crowds lined up outside the executive mansion and made his way back across Lafayette Square to his home. There, he spent the day in solitude. It was one of his few respites from the stress and exhaustion of working twelve hours a day and the irritating political intrigues that seemed never to end among cabinet members and leaders of the military. There was much to occupy Welles as January progressed and bad tidings for the U.S. Navy came one after another. At times, the strain became almost too much for him to bear.

Chapter Four

BOLD ESCAPE

Mobile Bay, January 15, 1863

Long, regular swells born of a southeasterly gale rolled across the broad expanse of the Gulf of Mexico toward the shallows off the spit of Mobile Point and the shores of the outlying islands to the west. As the seas met the resistance of the sandy bottom, they grew tall and irregular, rising up until their backs broke and tons of water toppled in cascades of foam. The wind blew straight down the main channel leading across the bar into the triangular confines of Mobile Bay beyond the Confederate-held Fort Morgan at the eastern approach. The seven Union warships anchored at the mouth of the bay surged backward against their anchor cables with each passing crest and thundered into the troughs before meeting the next wave. Their bows pointed out to sea. No land diminished the strength of the elements that had for many weeks past appeared benevolent, favoring the sailors and their officers with relative warmth and an ability to keep a sharp lookout for the rebel steamship they knew was intent upon escape.

Down below in his cabin, Commander George F. Emmons of blockader *R. R. Cuyler* steadied himself against the violent pitching of his vessel as he checked once again the reading on the barometer. He tapped the glass with his index finger to limber the needle. The low-pressure system had been stalled over the fleet for three days, but it was about to move. His log of barometric readings indicated a downward trend in pressure. In the last hour, between 9:00 a.m. and 10:00 a.m., the needle dropped precipitously.

Emmons went back on deck and ordered his officers to check the lashings on the gun batteries to insure that the heavy cannons could not break loose. He took bearings on the ruins of the lighthouse on Sand Island, Fort Morgan, and the sea buoy at the end of the main channel to determine if the ship remained on station, her anchor holding against the force of the storm. For the moment, all appeared secure. The day passed and as he expected the wind clocked round in a matter of hours more than ninety degrees, coming in from the west with increased strength. The vessels now pointed westward toward the outer islands. The swell from the prolonged southeasterly roared in as usual, creating a hideous roll as a cross-sea developed. Some of the green sailors of the squadron, and there were many of them, felt weak from seasickness.

In the waning light of the afternoon, visibility improved somewhat and a strange vessel caught the attention of the lookouts posted in the tops. They shouted to *Cuyler*'s officers on watch. Emmons was soon on deck, his glass in hand. He trained the lens on the low, dark steamship making way slowly down the bay. She came to anchor inside and to the east of Fort Morgan, her captain seeking shelter in the lee of the fortress, but with little effect. Bark-rigged, with two funnels, she was undoubtedly *Oreto* (*Florida*), the ship that had cost George Preble his career. Many of the officers considered his dismissal unjust, and many complained quietly among themselves about the way it was done. However, the swift and decisive action of Gideon Welles instilled in them a heightened sense of vigilance to avoid his anger. In moments, signals from *Cuyler* alerted the rest of the fleet.

Aboard USS *Susquehanna,* flagship of the blockading squadron, Commodore R. B. Hitchcock observed the rebel steamer through his glass, convinced her captain would try to escape under cover of the storm. *Florida* had tried several times to break out. It was so important to the U.S. Navy to keep her penned at Mobile, ensuring that she could not destroy valuable merchant vessels on the high seas, that a large number of warships sealed the port, drawing off naval assets needed elsewhere. Her counterpart, *Alabama,* was doing great damage to merchantmen, and no one wanted to see another pirate loose. In weeks past, as many as thirteen vessels blockaded the bay. Hitchcock ordered the ships under his command to tighten formation, signaling "Oreto expected out; keep full steam." Taking no chances that his orders might be misunderstood, Hitchcock dispatched one of the ships stationed nearby to steam over to *Cuyler* and *Oneida,* two of the fastest cruisers in the squadron, to come within hailing distance and inform the captains that they were to be the chasing vessels if the rebel came out. All precautions taken, the commanders and their officers settled in for the long night ahead. The lookouts were changed often because of the cold. After dark, the wind continued to shift, coming in from the west-northwest and bringing with it frigid temperatures and driving rain in squalls that reduced visibility to twenty yards.

While the men on blockade duty peered into the storm, wondering when the rebel might come and fighting their discomfort and the fatigue of waiting, *Florida*'s crew of approximately 160 men prepared to make good their escape. The ship hummed with excitement. For weeks the men had been restless, anxious to pursue their mission. Among the most impatient of them all was Second Lieutenant Charles W. Read. He repeatedly urged Maffitt to go out, to the point where Maffitt expressed his irritation at the man in his journal. "Our tarry has far exceeded my expectations, and all hands are very restive. Lieutenant Read suffers particularly in this and has become somewhat bilious. Every passing squall is to him a fine night for going out, even though it be of 50 minutes duration only."

Read was young and inexperienced, as were the bulk of the junior officers aboard *Florida*. In his journal, Maffitt gave his impressions of these men, speaking highly of Lieutenant E. D. Simms and Lieutenant

Samuel W. Averett, who was to serve as *Florida*'s second in command. However, he reported that Second Assistant Engineer Jackson was "a perfect bag of wind, devoid of modesty and ability," and that Lieutenant Comstock was a "young officer of exceeding delicacy of constitution, in fact unfitted for the performance of the requirements of this vessel."

Of all the men to receive comment from Maffitt, passages related to Read were the most lengthy:

Nov. 4 [1862] — Lieut. C. W. Read joined — this last lieutenant I personally applied for. He had acquired a reputation for gunnery, coolness and determination at the battle of New Orleans. When his commander, T. B. Huger, was fatally wounded he continued gallantly to fight the McRae until she was riddled and unfit for service. I am sorry to say the Government has not requited him. He seems slow — I doubt not but he is sure. As a military officer of the deck he is not equal to many — time will remedy this.

A veteran of the U.S. Navy at the age of forty-three, having received his commission as a midshipman when he was thirteen, Maffitt was something of a father figure to his men. They admired him, looked to him for guidance. For his part, Maffitt realized from his long years in the Navy that only time at sea and in action could bring together a group of men endowed with diverse and unique talents, individual weaknesses and strengths. He was prepared to give them the benefit of the doubt, until they proved either their worth or detriment to the ship. It was his mission, in the words of Secretary of the Confederate Navy Stephen R. Mallory, to "do the enemy's commerce the greatest injury in the shortest time." Maffitt understood that success depended on forming a cohesive fighting unit, and in the tactics of the commercial war victory depended more on forethought and cunning than bold action.

Through the night the storm raged and the men of both Confederate and Union navies waited. While some of the sailors tried to rest, the coal heavers at work in the fire rooms sweated in heat that was welcome, as they stoked the furnaces to keep steam up for any action that might come. The lookouts strained to see, but all appeared invisible, except the shadowy form of their vessel's hull, all ports blacked out to hide from the enemy. At around 2:30 a.m. on January 16, Commander Emmons retired below to the comfort of his cabin. He shrugged off his wet clothes and prepared for bed. The storm seemed to have moderated somewhat. The jagged rents in the clouds above the fleet revealed a clear sky spangled with the pricks of starlight. He contented himself with the thought that the most advantageous time for the rebel to make her run had passed. Other officers in the squadron concluded the same and went below, leaving the deck watch in charge of their junior officers.

Unseen in the light mist blowing across the warm waters of the bay, *Florida* steamed ahead slowly. The low sand spit of Mobile Point was hidden in the murk, but the shadow of Fort Morgan rose dark above the layer of fog. Sailors on deck stood ready at the halyards, sheets, and braces to set and trim sail on Maffitt's orders. The sails were double-reefed to reduce their size in the still-boisterous wind, and tied in loose furls to the yards with split rope yarns that would break free under pressure when the men on deck yanked hard on the lines. This method allowed for spreading canvas without sending men aloft to unfurl the topsails, a time-consuming and dangerous endeavor were *Florida* to take fire from the squadron waiting just outside the bar at the end of the main channel. The ship was painted a lead color, formed from a mixture of whitewash seasoned with lampblack, to help her merge with the night. Down below in the fire room, the heavers shoveled clean-burning anthracite coal into the furnaces. Anthracite did not produce much smoke, and tended to spark much less than inferior grades. There was little of it aboard.

The pilot steered *Florida* carefully around the tip of Mobile Point and turned southward down the main channel. She rolled heavily in the confused seas, and water surged over the weather deck through the open gunports. Every twenty feet or so, one of *Florida*'s junior officers stood watch at the bulwarks, braced against the violent motion of the vessel. They were to pass word to the helm should they sight a blockader. A ship loomed from the fog close aboard. The men on deck tensed. She was close. Very close. In moments, the Union ship dropped astern, then another appeared. The enemy surrounded *Florida*. For Read, it was a familiar situation. Twice before, at the Battle of New

Orleans and aboard *Arkansas*, he had served on a Confederate ship caught in the midst of a hostile fleet. Like those times, by all accounts he welcomed the excitement. Battle to him was a deadly game to be played in an active, aggressive manner. That *Florida* was now underway came as a pleasure and a harbinger of future glory for the Confederacy.

Florida drew past the second blockader, increasing speed as she closed with the terminus of the main channel and the open sea beyond. A third Union vessel hove dimly into view and as the ship came abeam a shower of red embers lit the top of *Florida*'s funnels and blew quickly to leeward. It became obvious to all that the scanty supply of anthracite had gone, and at the worst possible moment. Another cloud of sparks erupted from the stacks, and the night suddenly glowed with the flare of signal lights. The sound of drums carried on the wind as the Union sailors beat to quarters.

Commander Emmons had just settled into a fitful sleep when a rapid knocking on his stateroom door jolted him awake. The junior officer on watch standing before him reported as coolly as his self-control allowed "a vessel passing between [*Cuyler*] and [*Susquehanna*], which he supposed to be the *Oreto*, but could only see two masts."

"Beat to quarters immediately!" Emmons said. "Haul fires, prepare to slip, and burn private Coston signal No. 3 [white and green lights denoting steamer running out.]."

Only partially dressed, Emmons arrived on deck a few moments later as the crew forward slipped the anchor cable and *Cuyler* turned to bring her bow to the stern of the escaping steamer. All these actions took less than ten minutes. The rebel had set all sail and sped ahead fast. Emmons ordered all ahead full and all sail set. The wind blew off the starboard quarter and filled the sails one by one with a loud rush and bang. *Susquehanna* drew abeam and disappeared in the darkness, as did the rest of the fleet, save for the red, green, and white signal lights and the stab of search lamps. Ahead, *Florida*'s sails revealed her presence. The distance between them opened. As impossible a speed as it seemed, it appeared that *Florida* was making close to fourteen knots through the heavy seas, her decks almost constantly awash.

Astern of *Cuyler*, the light of another Union vessel gleamed in the darkness.

Thinking she was *Oneida*, Emmons signaled her to sail to the southward off his starboard quarter to cut off the rebel should she change course. He ordered a light hoisted aloft to enable the other chase vessel to keep him in sight, and to distinguish him from the enemy. Ahead, the sea and sky merged into a singular blackness broken only by flashes of phosphorescence churned up from the breaking crests. As time passed, Emmons became aware of the subtle change in the motion of his ship. She cruised farther from land into deep water. The seas increased in size, but she rolled less as the period between waves lengthened.

At dawn, the rebel steamed approximately five miles off *Cuyler's* bow. All about the sea broke from horizon to horizon. Neither land nor the squadron was in sight, and the second chase vessel turned back for Mobile a short while later. When larger groups of waves came in under the stern, lifting it skyward, the propeller raced clear of the water and shook the ship. The noise alarmed some of the sailors, and it did not sit well with Emmons either. It was not good to run the engine full out in such conditions. He noted that the masts bent forward under the pressure of the wind in the sails. The rigging stretched tight. The timbers groaned and worked. Water flowed into the bilge from the seams in the planking, a common occurrence in a heavy sea for even a sound vessel. *Cuyler's* hull, however, was in poor shape. Long duty on blockade meant a necessary but dangerous deferral of routine maintenance. The ship labored hard and still he could not ease her.

"Sails ho! Broad on the starboard beam!" the lookouts shouted.

In the distance, two Union troop ships loaded with men and ammunition struggled to windward under close-reefed topsails. They buried their bows deep in the seas and upon rising sent sheets of spray flying aft across their weather decks high enough to darken the lower edges of the sails. Emmons had no doubt the Confederates had seen the transports as well, the Stars and Stripes snapping to the gale. It pleased him that these ships at least were safe because of his close proximity to *Florida*. The rebel had no time to attack while he pursued her.

"Under all steam and sail that I could raise, I continued the chase all day in a combing sea that kept the decks covered with water and the propeller racing part of the time, sometimes gaining and at others losing; carried away topsail yard and had to send it down with the sail; had no substitute," Emmons later wrote in one of several official reports to his superiors. *Cuyler* slowed, and it seemed the race was lost. However, as daylight began to fade in late afternoon the gale moderated and in the smoother seas *Cuyler* drew to within three miles of the chase.

Florida's crew was aware that their enemy appeared ready to open fire, that she inevitably would send shot and shell their way in a short time when the range permitted. The nearness of the Union ship therefore added great urgency to the pressing business taking place high up on the foremast as the topmen struggled to send down the fore topsail yard that had just sprung under the immense loads from the wind and pitching of the hull. These were the most experienced sailors in the ship's company, the elite of the forecastle. The safety of the cruiser rested on their skill and courage. Unlike the topmen, very few of *Florida*'s hands could pass muster as able-bodied seamen. Most were recruits from the Confederate Army. Many were Irish and Scots with no knowledge of the sea, and some of them shipped because they were starving in the South and did not abide the suicidal tendency of soldiers to stand in lines of formation on an open battlefield exposed to volleys of minie balls, grapeshot, and explosive shells. They correctly deemed service on a commerce destroyer a much safer assignment.

The topmen worked furiously to remove the sail, their feet perched on the ropes beneath the yard, their bellies to the spar. They hauled the flogging canvas upward while the wind forced it toward the bow. Blood spattered the sail from the torn skin of their hands. At last, the sail was sent down, and next the yard. On deck, under the supervision of the ship's carpenter, crewmen coiled lines around it to draw the split wood together. The Union warship closed in with every passing minute. The men glanced aft and could just make out the enemy crew on deck at the bow gun. When the work was done and her canvas was restored, *Florida* picked up speed. The men cheered as they left their pursuer astern.

Maffitt was not content to spend another night running at full speed with a heavily armed enemy vessel in the wake. Should another failure to the rig occur, he might lose his ship. Only two Confederate commerce destroyers haunted the sea lanes. If he were sunk or captured, it would mean a great blow to the Southern cause, and an almost certain end to his career as an officer in the Confederate Navy. In the twilight, all hands set to taking in sail, and "like snow-flakes under a summer sun, our canvas melt[ed] from view . . . Thus shorn of her plumage, the engines at rest, between high toppling seas, clear daylight was necessary to enable them to distinguish [us]," Maffitt wrote. Lying in the trough, waves broke over the windward side of the ship and when she rolled deep green water rushed through the open gunports to leeward. The men clung to lifelines rigged fore and aft, and waited, the form of the enemy vessel obscured in the distance.

Cuyler's lookouts shouted, "Lost sight of the chase!"

Emmons looked at his watch in the light of the binnacle. It was 6:32 p.m. He zigzagged and backtracked, but could not find the rebel. He was cognizant of what *Florida*'s escape might mean to his career and to any American merchantmen unlucky enough to meet her. "From fancying myself near promotion in the morning, I gradually dwindled down to a court of enquiry at dark, when I lost sight of the enemy." He set his course for the shores of Cuba, hoping to intercept *Florida* there. But he never saw the Confederate pirate again.

Aboard *Florida* the men "jubilantly bid the enemy good-night and steer[ed] merrily to the southward." Perhaps the best description of the overall sentiments of the officers and crew on this day were expressed in the private journal of a landsman from Texas, A. L. Drayton, who had volunteered for service on the raider the previous autumn. "This ever memorable day has at last arrived and behold, this afternoon we [are] on the briny deep to fulfill the part assigned us in this war of justice and right on our side against fanaticism, injustice and oppression on the other. Our mission is to burn, sink and destroy all vessels that may wear the bunting of the United States."

Florida sailed on through the night, running before the wind on a southeasterly course, making good more than one hundred miles before dawn. As the sun rose over the Gulf of Mexico, the wind blowing just a fresh breeze and the seas subsiding, the midshipmen perched high aloft cried out, "Nothing in sight but sky and water!" Maffitt set the regular watches. Those off

91

duty went below to their berths, exhausted and yet well pleased that their adventure on the high seas had begun and yearning for the hour when a vessel showing the Stars and Stripes should heave into view on the distant horizon.

Chapter Five

CIVILIZED PIRATES

At Sea, 180 Miles Southeast of Cape Hatteras, February 6, 1863

Lieutenant Maffitt sat below at the desk in his small, dark cabin, a chart of the offshore waters of the United States spread before him. In the dim light cast from the lamp swaying to the pitch of the vessel, creating a dance of shadow on the chart, he examined the sweep of the coast — its barrier islands, the sounds behind them, and the shoals that stretched well to seaward. He had served in the Coast Survey making charts for the Navy. This work over sixteen years represented his longest duty assignment while serving the Union, and in its execution he acquired a better than average appreciation for the science of hydrography and navigation. Born at sea on February 22, 1819, aboard an immigrant ship bound from

Dublin to New York, he was most at home on the vast reaches of the deep, where the routine of life revolved around the weather and whatever good or bad fortune it might bring. He understood as he checked his calculations that a wise mariner knew when the elements demanded surrender.

Above him on the quarter deck two men struggled at the helm to keep *Florida* on course. Only the lashings that held them in place at the binnacle prevented their certain deaths in the event a breaking wave washed them overboard. Other men on watch at their sail stations frequently found themselves waist deep in swirling water as the ship buried her bow in the trough of an oncoming wave. The triple-reefed sails aloft bellied to the wind. The engines turned the propeller in slow revolutions, but not enough to make much way.

Maffitt's calculations involved more than simply deducing his whereabouts from the ship's speed, course, and time traveled between fixes, the influence of drift to leeward from the wind and waves, and the confounding eddies of the Gulf Stream not far to the west. The storm, if anything, appeared to be intensifying, and he entertained the uneasy thought that it was not a typical gale but a rare winter cyclone. Hurricanes were not supposed to occur when the weather was cool and the waters held less heat than in summer, when the Caribbean became as hot as a piping bath. Yet, the warm waters of the Gulf Stream and the capricious nature of weather did strange things. Thus, his calculations extended beyond mere dead reckoning and an accounting of how much coal he had burned in his attempt to reach the coast of New England. He analyzed the series of wind shifts and the types of clouds he observed since February 2, after he cleared Great Abaco Island in the Bahamas and stood northward.

Dried salt peppered the mat of his full black beard and stung his eyes. Moisture soaked his heavy clothing and caused his skin to itch. The voyage had just begun, yet he was already tired. Mechanical difficulties with the engines, inferior coal, the desertion of twenty-six men in Havana, and almost running hard aground on the Bahama Bank were just a few of the travails he and his officers dealt with since their escape from Mobile. The Union ships hunting for him and *Alabama* also created excitement on two occasions. USS *Sonoma* chased him for more than three hundred miles before he eluded her off Great Abaco Island on February 2. The previous night, he had encountered a second Union cruiser. She sighted him and ranged close, emerging from the storm at high speed. She sparked great anxiety among all those aboard *Florida*. "I am convinced that 'twas the Vanderbilt, and we deceived her by a small light, mistaking us for some West India trader. To have been rammed by this immense steamer would have closed our career, and all were rejoiced to see her leave us."

She was indeed USS *Vanderbilt*, en route to the waters off Brazil in search of *Alabama*, under special orders from Gideon Welles. Built for Cornelius Vanderbilt at a cost of nearly $1 million, she was for a time the world's largest passenger liner in the late 1850s, displacing close to five thousand tons and extending 355 feet on deck. She was typical of Vanderbilt's tendency to build big and grand, and a result of the intense rivalry between Vanderbilt and Edward Knight Collins, manager of the ill-fated Collins Line, which went bankrupt in 1858. Like *Vanderbilt*, two of the three Collins liners still afloat, *Baltic* and *Atlantic*, went into service for the Union during the American Civil War. These were just some of the famous ships Welles chartered in his effort to build up the Navy.

All reports indicated both rebel commerce destroyers were in Caribbean waters and headed eastward. Accounts in the newspapers told of *Alabama*'s victory in the Gulf of Mexico on January 11, off Galveston, Texas, when she engaged and sank USS *Hatteras*. Preceding these were stories of how Galveston fell to a combined attack of the Confederate Army and Navy on New Year's Day, an embarrassing defeat for Welles, and how the turreted ironclad *Monitor* foundered off Cape Hatteras on New Year's Eve. *Florida*'s exploits received headlines in the most recent spate of reportage, and the string of naval disasters led to increased criticism of Welles in the press. He was forced to take *Vanderbilt* from transport duty to hunt for the rebel pirates.

A highly critical story published in the *New York Times* on January 30 read in part:

The Navy Department has now, we are told, determined to send the Vanderbilt on this work instead of employing her as a transport. If she had been for the last month where common sense dictated she should be, we might now have been rid of the Alabama, and the Florida might have lain rotting in the harbor of Mobile. We have known all along where the Florida was; we knew her character and her purpose; we knew she was watching her chance to come out. Commander Preble was dismissed the service for allowing her to run into Mobile five months ago; is it not time that the higher functionary who is really responsible for her escape, was also dismissed the service? As for our British friends who furnished the Florida, as they did also the Alabama, to the rebels, and our Spanish-Cuban friends, who are doing all they can to aid them in their work of destruction, we shall be better able to apply a remedy to their delinquencies and crimes when we have corrected our own.

The same article provided details on the three ships *Florida* sank shortly after her escape: *Estelle, Windward,* and *Corris Ann.* It went on to predict further depredations.

All this was precisely one week's work; how many more of our vessels this piratical rover may have captured and burnt during the seven days that have elapsed since the 23d, we shall probably not be long in knowing. From the statements made [by those captured and later released in neutral ports], it would appear that the Florida is quite as fast a sailer as her compeer, the Alabama, and it is evident that Capt. Maffit is as venturesome a knave as Capt. Semmes. Of course the capturing and burning of unarmed and unsuspecting trading craft in the West India waters is not a work that contains in it a single characteristic of courage, or that requires much skill.

Whatever the reporters might have thought of the lack of skill involved in operating a commerce destroyer, it was not an accurate assessment. It required both a flair for international diplomacy and the daring of a pirate to steam in shipping lanes subject to regular patrols of Union cruisers. It required cunning as well. In sailing north, Maffitt had placed his ship where no Union commander expected to find her. However, he now had to make a difficult decision. Should he sail on under the present circumstances, with a severe storm raging about him and with a depleted supply of coal?

Florida staggered after a particularly heavy sea boarded over the forecastle deck. Maffitt waited for her to rise. He heard torrents of water rush overhead, so loud that it almost drowned out the scream of the wind in the rigging. She got her footing and pushed on, in spite of the mounting damage to her rig and sails and the terrible strain on the engines. The seas tore one of the rowboats from the lashings and swept it over the side. Having completed his calculations, Maffitt confirmed that the ship was caught on the most dangerous side of the hurricane, the northeast quadrant in which the forward motion of the storm added to the wind speed around its center. Conditions would only worsen. On her current heading, Florida traveled with the storm and prolonged her time in it by doing so. He made his decision. Later, he wrote in his journal:

Stood to the northward [from Abaco], with the view of giving the coast of New England a small appreciation of war troubles, but a gale off Cape Hatteras did us much injury and our coal was low, for the Florida, unfortunately, stows but nine days' full steaming coal. Had to run southward and eastward to get out of the circle of the gale. It was a cyclone of considerable power. The Florida behaved well, though exceedingly wet. It was evident now that I would have to enter a West India port for coal, etc. Deeply did I regret my inability to make the anticipated visit.

The sixth of February marked the apex of a pyramid on Maffitt's chart. His plots ranged northward in a near-straight line, then slanted off across the top of the Bahamas well above these islands. The ship passed to the north of Hispanola and reached a position approximately three hundred miles due north of Puerto Rico on February 12. The tropical sun heated the deck and softened the tar on the standing rigging. Men set to their routine of scraping paint, greasing the topmasts to enable the yards to run freely, and working the slack from the shrouds at the deadeyes. Sextant in hand, an assistant at his side to mark the ship's local time when he commanded, Maffitt prepared to take his forenoon sun sight. A cry from aloft halted routine duty and all the men on deck observed the skysails of a large ship just visible on the horizon. At Maffitt's orders, the topmen crowded on studding sails. The firemen hauled fires to make ready for full steam. The coal heavers, stripped to their pantaloons and already covered in sweat, grabbed their shovels and shifted the last of the coal from the rear of the bunkers to the front, where they could better access it in a hurry.

The clipper ship *Jacob Bell* glided through the easy swells approximately three hundred miles due north of Puerto Rico, making eight knots in a diminishing breeze. She was bound from Foochow, China, to the port of New York laden with 1,380 tons of tea; camphor; 10,000 crates of fireworks; and other cargo valued in excess of $1.5 million. The China tea clippers were among the fastest and most valuable ships in the U.S. Merchant Marine. Although the immense profits of the mid-1850s were gone, these vessels still inspired pride in those with a keen appreciation for their beauty and a longing for a return to the prosperity that marked the opening of the previous decade. Her passengers lounged on deck under the shade of awnings — reading, sitting quietly, or playing cards as they passed the time on yet another monotonous day at sea. All looked forward to reaching their destination after so long an absence from home.

It had been five months since the passengers and crew received news from the United States. They had not yet heard about the battles of Antietam in September, Fredericksburg in December, and Murfreesboro in January. Likewise, Captain Frisbie, master of *Jacob Bell*, knew nothing of *Alabama* or *Florida*. When his lookout sighted a vessel astern at around noon, he paid little attention. As the hours passed, and she drew nearer under full sail, the black smoke blowing off to leeward revealed that she was a fast steamer making directly for them. Still, he did not worry. He thought it likely that she was a Union gunboat because she flew the Stars and Stripes at her peak, and he welcomed the opportunity to hail her and obtain newspaper reports on the war.

Seated in a comfortable chair on the poop deck not far from the officers of the clipper was Mrs. Dwight H. Williams, wife of the Commissioner of Customs at Swatow, China. Williams was in the employ of the Chinese Imperial government and charged with the collection of duties from American vessels calling at the port. As such, he was an important man and his wife, an educated woman, felt herself entitled to the privileges associated with her husband's rank. She fanned herself under the hot sun and watched with pleasant anticipation the ship steaming toward them.

However, as the steamer approached, she noted that Captain Frisbie exhibited signs of unease. He constantly lifted his glass to survey the stranger.

Frisbie turned to his first officer and ordered the American flag unfurled and set flying from the peak of the mizzen gaff. It fluttered in the gentle breeze, making a fine sight. The gun on the steamer's bow boomed in the distance, about three miles astern, and in another second a column of white water shot skyward approximately three hundred fifty feet off the clipper's port quarter. It was a well aimed shot at maximum range, quite possibly fired by Read, one of *Florida*'s best gunners. All aboard the clipper stared aft in utter disbelief. The captain brought *Jacob Bell*'s head to wind, backing topsails and taking in staysails, understanding all too well the intentions of the low, rakish craft running down on them at flank speed.

"We had not thought of being molested by southern pirates," Williams later wrote. ". . . The firing of the gun sent me directly into the cabin; but, through Master Charlie [a youth traveling alone], I learned that in about ten minutes after I had left the deck, the steamer, which proved to be the *Florida*, — a pirate, officered and manned by the rebels of the Southern States, — came round our stern to the port side, and when within two ship's lengths of us ran up the rebel Confederate flag, — taking down the 'stars and stripes' — and hailed us."

A longboat put off from *Florida* full of armed men. They clambered up the side of the clipper and the officer in charge strode aft to Captain Frisbie, the passengers and crew watching from the weather deck. "You are a prize of the Confederate States of America!" the officer said.

"But this is English property," Frisbie said.

"I can't help that. I must obey my orders."

"Is this the way you take English property on the high seas?"

"Yes, sir," the officer said. "Lord John Russell has recently said that if English subjects put their property in United States vessels, they must look for pay to the Confederate government. You will go aboard the steamer with your papers, sir."

"What of the passengers and crew?"

"All must go aboard. Your private property will be saved, but after we are finished taking what we need, we will burn this ship."

The people of *Jacob Bell* rushed to gather a few belongings from their cabins and the transfer began, starting with the crew, all of whom were disarmed upon arriving aboard *Florida* and forced to sign a pledge stating that they would not attack the ship's company. The two ladies, Mrs. Williams and Frisbie's pregnant wife, were lashed into a chair together and hoisted over the side of the clipper into a boat waiting below. The hoisting process was repeated once the boat reached *Florida*.

". . . To be re-hoisted . . . and lowered upon the deck of an armed vessel prepared for piratical warfare, amid the gaze of brutalized and vicious men, whose vulgar, jeering expression of countenance was enough to make any one shrink back involuntarily with loathing and indignation, was a severe test for a woman. . . ."

Maffitt strode forward from the quarter deck and escorted the ladies aft to his cabin, offering his private stateroom to one of them for the duration of their stay in what Mrs. Williams described as "the patronizing, host-like air of one about offering the most agreeable hospitality." Maffitt hurried away, for another sail loomed over the horizon and he set to a new chase, leaving *Jacob Bell* in the possession of a prize crew. The prisoners watched as *Florida* pursued the Union ship, and rejoiced when she disappeared from sight as dusk turned to night and the rebel cruiser was alone once again under a sky filled with stars strangely beautiful in a time of great distress. *Jacob Bell* sailed unseen somewhere, and her people wondered if she might yet be spared were she to not fall in with her captors at dawn.

These hopes, though, were to no avail. The following morning the two ships came together again and the plundering began. According to Mrs. Williams, although Maffitt later denied it, private property was taken, a violation of the rules governing the conduct of commerce destroyers. Each side clearly despised the other, and the truth of what happened as the morning progressed probably resided somewhere between the two accounts. Maffitt described Mrs. Williams as "something of a tartar" and added: "If they speak unkindly, such a thing as gratitude is a stranger to their abolition hearts." Mrs. Williams singled Maffitt out in her report of her encounter with *Florida* and her men. She gave a most damning view of him as a man and a father:

He [Maffitt] also told us of a letter written by his youngest son, in which the hopeful youth requested his father to 'send him a Yankee's head with the teeth all in!!!' . . . . None of us dared to give utterance to the thoughts suggested on hearing of so savage a request from such a child, — if, indeed, the child ever made it; — and it is difficult to think that Christendom, in this age of the world, is capable of producing a father willing thus to advertise the disgustingly precocious ferocity of his little son. The bloody request indicated the Nero-like training to which the child had been subjected, and the malicious hatred he was already capable of bearing towards his kind. If this is the child, what will be the horrid proportions of the man?

Mrs. Williams also singled Read out in her account. As the officers and men shuttled all manner of goods from *Jacob Bell* to their ship, Williams watched with quiet rage.

The *officers* [her emphasis] of the *Florida* — the so-called boasted *chivalry* of the South — were now shamelessly enacting the burglar and shop-lifter, directly before my eyes; and carrying my property in tumbled, confused masses, — some of it dragging and trailing on the deck, — into their ward-room. I saw Lieutenant Reed with a huge armful of cotton-sheeting and unmade table-linen, — grasping at the same time in one hand my cake-basket, (the wrappers of which being torn off it was exposed to my gaze,) — rush from the side of the ship to the ward-room entrance; when seeing that I was watching him in mute astonishment, he dropped his eyes and hurried below like a detected thief. This scene of pillage continued for several hours.

Aboard *Jacob Bell*, young Charlie witnessed similar activities. He had been allowed to go back aboard to retrieve belongings he had left behind in the rush of the previous afternoon, but upon arriving at the clipper he was prevented from recovering his only possessions. He described the occurrences to Williams, and although perhaps amusing to a modern reader, they did not strike the boy as funny at all. "One officer was seen examining and helping himself from a box of fans, — taking them out one by one, and fanning himself, to see which he liked the best. Another laid hold of a hoop-skirt, and putting it on, tripped over the main-deck with a grace and delicacy doubtless unattainable except by a representative of Southern *chivalry!*"

The impact of the events of the previous day and witnessing the actions of the Confederate sailors aboard *Jacob Bell* instilled in Charlie bitter anger. The son of a missionary, Williams described him as gentle. Yet, when he returned to *Florida* he said: "I never was so mad in all my life! O! It was a fearful scene; I shall never forget it." Later, still seething, he said: "I hope yet to meet them with a gun in my hand!"

The sailors aboard the Confederate raiders never killed a single individual throughout the duration of the war. (A New England coastal steamer was hijacked, and some of her company murdered by the rebel highjackers.) Their actions were nevertheless perceived as terrorism from the Northern point of view. The destruction of property and ships, and the feelings of the victims subjected to these "outrageous depredations," were well reported in the newspapers. The commerce destroyers, while fighting the United States on an economic front, also were quite effective tools of psychological warfare. The Confederate officers did not necessarily view it as such, as modern generals who employ "psy-ops" as an instrument of war, but it amounted to the same thing and accomplished the desired objective of frightening the public. In addition, it fanned the hatred of many Northern citizens for their fellow Americans in the South, and helped to widen the gap between both sides.

The Confederate sailors spent most of February 13 engaged in their work aboard *Jacob Bell*. At around four in the afternoon, they set the clipper on fire. *Florida* got underway. Smoke billowed from the hatches and soon the people gathered on the raider's decks noticed flames. The tar on the shrouds and stays caught fire, and the flames traveled up the rigging to ignite the sails. The fireworks in the hold exploded, the reports rumbling over the ocean like claps of thunder. The ship drifted farther away, transformed into a "pyramid of fire."

To us the last sight of our noble ship a little before her masts fell, when with her sails and rigging all a-blaze, she was quietly floating on, impressed us with a scene of awful and melancholy grandeur. The sublimity of such a spectacle depends altogether on the circumstances under which we behold it. Our ideas of things are merely relative, and depend for their moral effect upon the power of association. Hence, the contemplation of any wide-spread ruin may be the height of the sublime to a disinterested spectator; but to another, whose worldly interests, or, as was feared in this instance, whose life is depending upon the character and extent of the calamity, it can be nothing else than a scene of horror and dismay.

Smoke from the clipper rose above the sea as she continued to burn down to her waterline. It took time for the fire to completely destroy her and the water to flow inside the vessel to finally end the display. The evidence of her destruction lingered on the gentle breeze for hours, until the sun sank low on the western horizon and night fell quickly, as it does in the tropics. *Florida* sailed on, the fires in her furnaces banked to preserve coal. She headed to the southeast, across the top of the northern islands of the Caribbean, then turned to a more southerly course. Her sharp bow pointed in the direction of Barbados and a renewed supply of coal that would allow her to inspire more terror among Yankees traveling on the high seas.

Chapter Six

FOREIGN THREAT

Navy Department, Washington, D. C., May 2, 1863

Early spring brought comforting relief from the cold to the men encamped in the fortifications surrounding Washington, and reminded the more fit of the soldiers that the balmy weather heralded a renewal of their marches south toward Richmond. It was an odd juxtaposition of cycles. Imminent death was ushered in with the seasonal restoration of life, so obvious from the budding trees and migratory birds returning to fill the woodlands and fields with song. At night, the hum of insects mingled with the crackle of the cook fires that flickered in orange looms around the city. The poorly paved streets became catches for hospital wagons and four-in-hand carriages alike, their iron-rimmed

113

wheels channeled into muddy ruts pooled with tepid rains. In the interior of the city, in its mansions and more modest dwellings, those possessing money enough prepared to depart before the summer humidity invited disease.

The change of seasons did little to relieve Gideon Welles. The weeks blended into a succession of disappointments, and a personal battle against fatigue and illness caused by too much work. Long subject to fits of melancholy, his quick mind too readily susceptible to an active sense of gloom, Welles at times became deeply depressed and hopelessly resigned to what it seemed might be an indefinite continuation of the struggle to preserve the Union. The press of business kept him at the Navy Department when he should have been at home resting.

In those dark moments, the progress the Navy had made did not hold much luster. However, the strategy to cut off the Confederacy and squeeze it tight was working. The taking of Hatteras Inlet and Port Royal in the first months of the war, the capture of Roanoke Island and Fort Donelson in February 1862, and establishing control of the upper and lower Mississippi River in April of that same year were all victories that contributed to generally weaken the South's hold on its heartland. The blockade was becoming more effective as the Navy grew to a fleet in excess of three hundred, and the ironclad warships based on the revolutionary design of USS *Monitor* ranked as some of Welles's prime achievements.

Nevertheless, the present difficulties overshadowed the successes. The attack on Charleston that Welles had worked for months to bring off failed in early April, and it caused him considerable consternation. Under heavy fire from the port defenses, the large fleet of ironclads and support ships retreated after what Welles viewed as a half-hearted assault under the direction of Admiral Samuel Du Pont. As an administrator, he relied on his senior officers to fight with daring and courage to carry out the plans he and his trusted advisers thought were worth pursuing. While many did, some lacked the proper zeal for their duty. Du Pont appeared to be one of the latter, and Welles blamed himself for not seeing the man's deficiencies long before the aborted Charleston offensive.

In conversations with Lincoln about the coming battle, the president often said he believed it would end badly, that Du Pont reminded him of George B. McClellan because of his constant requests for more military assets before he moved. In short, Lincoln said Du Pont had the "slows," a malady the president had previously reserved especially for McClellan. Welles saw the merit of Lincoln's assessment and prepared to relieve the admiral and put a better man in charge: "I fear that he [Du Pont] can be no longer useful in his present command, and am mortified and vexed that I did not earlier detect his vanity and weakness. They have lost us the opportunity to take Charleston, which a man of more daring energy and who had not a distinguished name to nurse and take care of would have improved."

In the west, the siege of Vicksburg continued, the army unable to advance against the stubborn enemy. And, on this day, rumors of more ill tidings regarding the latest forward movement of the Army of the Potomac and its concentration in the vicinity of Chancellorsville circulated widely through the city. As Welles worked on his papers and dispatches on the second day of May, General Stonewall Jackson was marching approximately twenty-six thousand men fourteen miles around the bulk of the Union Army in a bold and ultimately effective bid to outflank it, a decisive maneuver that added yet another staggering defeat to the list of botched battles in the land war. Rumors were common in Washington, and Welles tried to keep them from distracting him.

"I abstain from going to the War Department more than is necessary or consulting operators at the telegraph, for there is a hazy uncertainty there. This indefiniteness, and the manner attending it, is a pretty certain indication that the information received is not particularly gratifying."

On Welles's desk was a letter he just finished composing. He picked it up and frowned as he read the first few lines in his response to the governor of the state of Massachusetts, His Excellency John A. Andrew, a political rival who wanted Welles's job and often derisively referred to him as "that old Mormon deacon." The politician had clearly tried to get around him, going over his head directly to President Lincoln in his desire to pressure the Navy for protection of the New England coast against the rebel pirates who still roamed loose on the high seas. Although the list of burned vessels kept increasing, Welles refused to surrender to the impulse of panic that seemed so easily to attract others. The

West India Squadron hunted *Florida* and *Alabama*, and with luck the captains of these ships would find themselves under the guns of the U.S. Navy. Welles harbored a sometimes publicly stated hope to see them both hang for piracy. According to some in the government, the actions of these commerce destroyers exceeded the rules of international law, and most certainly went beyond the moral code of decency even in a time of war. They were ruthless buccaneers, nothing else, and if caught should be treated no better than common criminals.

However much he disliked it, Welles found himself in the position of having to placate Governor Andrew. President Lincoln expressed concerns about coastal defense, and had actually walked over to the Navy Department to discuss the issue with Welles on April 30. The president came with a letter from Andrew dated April 27. That very morning, Welles had just received one from the esteemed gentleman of Massachusetts along similar lines, dated April 28. Lincoln wanted something done. That was clear. Welles himself understood the unpleasant implications, both political and economic, should one of these pirates sweep in to destroy American shipping within sight of the busiest ports in the Northeast.

Governor Andrew wrote to Lincoln, saying among other things that "through Vineyard sound 90,000 vessels have been counted as passing Gay Head light in the course of twelve months." This figure was true, even if it included repeated passings of the same ships on their runs up and down the southern New England coast. It indicated just how fertile the hunting grounds of a Confederate commerce destroyer would be if one ever got so far north. Andrew further stated, in a direct poke at Welles, that "not a single Federal vessel of war cruises in Massachusetts Bay for the protection of its coast and commerce . . ." and that "The anxiety of this whole community [Boston and other coastal cities] for protection from sudden incursion by sea, the vast material interests at stake, and my own consciousness of the reasonable character of my request, unite to induce me to ask an early reply to this communication."

Andrew wanted a fast cruiser to patrol the coastal waters and an ironclad of the *Monitor* class to stand guard in Boston Harbor. He said so to Lincoln and repeated it to Welles. He also wrote a letter on April 28 to Massachusetts senator Charles Sumner asking him to facilitate the arming of the ship Ohio with a gun battery, and to order its crew to cruise the outer islands just off Boston Harbor and the channels leading to the city wharves. That Andrew was worried about pirates clearly came through in his letters.

Welles had received similar complaints and petitions from the men of the New York Chamber of Commerce, primarily those with a financial stake in maritime commerce. They thought a true sailor should administer the Navy Department, as opposed to a well-connected, career politician whom they believed had gotten the position out of Lincoln's sense of political patronage and need to include a New Englander in his cabinet. Though Welles never admitted it, they were not altogether incorrect. They were wrong, however, to assert that simply because he was not a sailor he was unfit to administer the Navy. He was suited for the post — honest, hard working, and forward thinking. One example of his foresight was his early conviction to develop the iron-clad known as the *Monitor*, in spite of opposition to the innovative design from naval officers steeped in the old ways of wooden sailing ships. He also shunned traditions that favored senior officers for almost automatic promotion, and assigned commands based on merit and an officer's willingness to fight.

Welles also received plenty of help from his able assistant, Gustavus Vasa Fox, who was an experienced seaman. A graduate of the Naval Academy at Annapolis, class of 1841, Fox served in the Mexican-American War and worked his way up from midshipman to lieutenant. Promotions were slow in coming in the 1850s, and seeing a better way to prosperity in the private sector, Fox resigned his commission in 1856 to go into business.

As the Civil War loomed in early 1861, Fox volunteered to lead an expedition to resupply Fort Sumter in Charleston, South Carolina, but failed to complete the mission. His work, however, brought him to the attention of President Lincoln, who became one of his chief supporters and often consulted him on naval matters. Fox was appointed chief clerk of the Navy Department on May 9, 1861, and on August 1 was elevated to the newly created position of assistant secretary of the navy. He was a major advocate of the *Monitor*, and he helped Welles form policies regarding personnel and procedures as the Navy Department grew from a sleepy little enclave to a large, busy organization during the war.

Like Welles's detractors in the New York Chamber of Commerce, some historians say it was Fox who ran the Navy Department, that he was the key player behind its ultimate success. However, a more accurate assessment is that between the two of them, Welles and Fox made a fine team, each bringing skills to the tasks at hand that the other lacked. Fox was never one to belittle his boss, but he did enjoy the praise he received from the very people Welles despised.

Welles's opinion of the New Yorkers, as expressed in his diary on January 3, 1863, reveals the extent to which he was bothered by his critics. He wrote: "There is a set of factious fools who think it is wise to be censorious, and it is almost as amusing as it is vexatious to hear and read the remarks of these Solomons. One or two of these officious blockheads make themselves conspicuous in the New York Chamber of Commerce. . . ." He felt the same way about men of that ilk up in Boston, though in replying to Andrew he resisted the urge to let him know his true sentiments.

The governor's concerted lobby effort to procure naval assets for the defense of the coast and the city of Boston marked the latest reactions among government officials and influential people in the mercantile community to the depredations of *Florida* and *Alabama*. There were others whose complaints had reached the Cabinet and the halls of Congress. Back in March, these two ships gave impetus to a congressional enactment of a law granting power to President Lincoln to "make all needful rules and regulations for the government and conduct of private armed vessels, furnished with letters of marque" that gave them official sanction from the United States to search for and destroy *Florida* and *Alabama*. They were also to "catch blockade runners."

Welles believed that Congress had abdicated its legislative responsibilities by wrongly conferring such powers on the executive. He considered it a dangerous precedent that defied the Constitution. The implications of the policy of issuing letters of marque greatly disturbed Welles for other reasons, too. Chief among them was his concern that it might spark a war with England. The issue caused him intense inner conflict regarding whether he should support the move or not.

On the night of April 2, President Lincoln visited Welles at home to discuss the idea of sending out privateers to augment the Navy's efforts. The two men sat together in Welles's drawing room and a lengthy conversation took place, with Lincoln for the most part listening while Welles spoke.

I started out with the proposition that to issue letters of marque would in all probability involve us in a war with England. [I said] that I had so viewed this question from the beginning, though he [Lincoln] and Mr. Seward had not; that I was not prepared to deny that it might not be best for us to move promptly with that object in view, though it had not yet been urged or stated; but that if we were to resort to letters of marque we should do it understandingly and with all the consequences before us.

The idea that private parties would send out armed ships to capture the *Alabama* and one, possibly two, other rovers of the Rebels was too absurd to be thought of for a moment. If privateers were fitted out for any purpose it would be to capture neutral vessels intended to run the blockade or supposed to be in that service. It was not difficult for us to foresee that such a power in private hands would degenerate into an abuse for which this Government would be held responsible. The Rebels have no commerce to invite private enterprise. So far as the Rebels were concerned, therefore, I had been opposed to committing the Government to the measure.

But the disclosures recently made had given a different aspect to the question. There was little doubt the British Government and British capital were encouraging the rebellion; that that Government intended to interpose no obstacle to prevent the sending out of privateers from British ports to depredate upon our commerce; that these privateers, though sailing under the Confederate flag, would be the property of British merchants; that the rich plunder would repay the lawless English adventurer, knowing he had the sanction of his Government; that this combination of British capital with Rebel malignity and desperation would despoil our commerce and drive it from the seas.

Our countrymen would not quietly submit to these wrongs and outrages, and allow Englishmen to make war upon us in disguise under the Rebel flag. We ought, therefore, to have an immediate and distinct understanding with the English Government. It should be informed in terms that could not be mistaken or misunderstood that if this policy was persisted in we should in self-defense be under the necessity of resorting to reprisals. In this view the law which authorized letters of marque had appeared to me proper, and might be made useful as a menace and admonition to England; and I repeated what I had said to the Secretary of State in reply to a remark of his that we must make more extensive naval operations against the Rebels by issuing letters of marque to annoy them, — that letters of marque, instead of annoying them, destitute as they were of commerce, would aid them, for that step would involve war with England. . . .

If the late dispatches are to be taken as the policy she intends to pursue, it means war, and if war is to come it looks to me as of a magnitude greater than the world has ever experienced, — as it would eventuate in the upheaval of nations, the overthrow of governments and dynasties. The sympathies of the mass of mankind would be with us rather than with the decaying dynasties and the old effete governments.

Not unlikely the conflict thus commenced would kindle the torch of civil war throughout Christendom, and even nations beyond. I desired no such conflict in my day, and therefore hoped and believed the policy and the tone of England might be modified, but it would require energy, resolution, and a firm determination on our part to effect it.

The President listened, for I did most of the talking, as he evidently wished, and showed much interest and accord in what I said. . . . It was evident I suggested some ideas that had not before occurred to him, and I am not without hope that the tone of our foreign affairs, particularly with England, may be different.

Welles's strong language in his diary outlining his concerns may well have been an exaggerated perception of the true nature of the threat the policy of issuing letters of marque might have brought about. Nevertheless, the friction between Britain and the United States was very real indeed, and it was not beyond the realm of imagination to see how war might have resulted had the policy gone into effect on a large scale. Discussions about whether to institute it dragged on through the spring. Lincoln was ambivalent as to what he should do. On the one hand, he wanted to rid the seas of the rebel commerce raiders. On the other, he wanted to avoid war with England.

In the end, the policy died on the vine. Welles was quite right to believe that Yankee merchants would see little opportunity to profit by arming ships and sending them after *Florida* and *Alabama*, only to face the distinct possibility that the rebels would blow them out of the water if they ever crossed paths. The merchants were not inclined to waste time and money on such a risky venture, nor were they inclined to invest in ships to pursue blockade runners. The liabilities outweighed the potential gains.

The law remained on the books. While it did not actually result in waves of American privateers sweeping the sea of British-backed blockade runners, the very fact that it had passed represented yet another sore point between the United States and Britain.

In April, the two nations clashed again, this time over the disposition of captured mails, an issue that had been festering for months. Welles dedicated pages of his diary to his belief that the disposition of captured foreign mails from ships caught running the blockade should be left up to the courts, per international law. Secretary of State Seward, seeking to placate the British, made commitments to the effect that the United States would return captured mails, unopened. The troubles arose over the British prize *Peterhoff*, which carried British mailbags the British government wanted back.

Welles's diary entry of April 22 clearly indicates his displeasure at the fact that, through exerting influence on President Lincoln, Seward was able to get his way in the matter. "The evening papers state that the mail of the Peterhoff has been given up by District Attorney Delafield Smith, who applied to the court under direction of the Secretary of State, 'approved' by the President. It is a great error, which has its origin in the meddlesome disposition and loose and inconsiderate action of Mr. Seward, who has meddlesomely committed himself [to return the captured mail]."

This was just one of many battles between Welles and Seward. It shows how nervous members of the Lincoln administration were about war with Britain, and how anxious they were to avoid one. Lincoln himself was bent on doing just about anything to stop a confrontation, no matter what happened. He finally resigned himself to accept the depredations of the commerce destroyers as part of the war, and pressured Welles to catch them as quickly as possible. He also gave in on the issue of the mails.

In addition to the issue of letters of marque and captured mails, the British protested the actions of Rear Admiral Charles Wilkes, commander of the West India Squadron. They cited numerous violations of the laws of neutrality in his pursuit of vessels suspected of blockade running as well as his ongoing search for *Florida* and *Alabama*. Wilkes was fond of searching any ship he suspected might be supporting the Confederates, and it often turned out that his squadron searched ships that were on legitimate business, greatly annoying the captains, who promptly registered an official complaint. The British threatened to retaliate. There was still more talk of war. A study of Welles's diary and official war records reveals that he battled two adversaries with equal zeal — the Confederates and the British. Each was capable of inflicting great harm on the United States. Together they might actually succeed in destroying what many people at home and abroad still termed the "great American experiment."

In November 1861, Wilkes stopped the British mail ship *Trent* and arrested Confederate agents James M. Mason and John Slidell, along with their two secretaries. He transported them to Fort Warren in Boston, and for a brief time his bold though technically illegal act earned him status as a national hero. Britain said it would go to war over the stopping of an official vessel of the British government on the high seas and forcibly removing passengers who were under its protection, the first of many such threats. They sent approximately eight thousand troops to Canada, and the British Atlantic fleet went on full alert. Ultimately, the United States was forced to release the Confederate prisoners, thus averting an armed conflict with England. However, the British remembered the Trent Affair, as it came to be called, and they took every opportunity to thwart Wilkes's efforts in the West Indies.

The letter from Governor Andrew, then, was just one more unpleasant consequence of the British backing of the Confederacy, and of the rebel pirates themselves as they went so efficiently about the business of destroying American shipping. From Welles's vantage point, being privy to all the details, he saw the bigger picture and how all the various elements comprising the landscape of the war on the high seas fit together. *Florida* and *Alabama* were causing more trouble than should have been accorded their actions, even pushing the United States into taking a measure such as issuing letters of marque that might mean war with England and sparking a global conflict that might last for a generation. Welles would not fall into the trap of overreacting, regardless of pressure from the president. He would do only what he thought was right under the circumstances.

Welles continued reading his letter to Andrew, satisfying himself that he had explained his reasons for denying deployment of an ironclad of the *Monitor* class to defend Boston Harbor. He also made sure to cover himself in the event the governor pursued his campaign with Lincoln. As for the fast cruiser, Welles wisely agreed with Andrew: "It has appeared to me that, to guard against the improbable but possible contingency of a hasty descent by one or more of these rovers upon some unprepared place upon the coast, it might be a wise precaution to have a fast cruiser stationed at Boston and always prepared for service. . . .

We can at this time ill spare one of our fast cruisers for such a service, but it may be a wise and advisable precaution demanded by the great population and interests involved. The Department will, therefore, make it a point to have a cruiser stationed at Boston." As a final tip to Andrew, throwing him a bone, Welles authorized arming *Ohio* for "additional security to Boston."

Perhaps Welles was justified in husbanding naval assets for what he believed were more important duties and in considering the fear of the pirates in Boston and New York overblown. After all, the latest reports from the West India Squadron placed both rebel cruisers in the waters off Brazil thousands of miles away from the Northeast. The Confederates would not dare to come north and risk the loss of their prized and much vaunted corsairs; such an attack would be foolish. If the Confederates had proven anything in this long war, it was that they were far from stupid. Welles called a clerk into his office and gave him the letter to Governor Andrew for copying. The clerk hurried away, and Welles did not give the matter much additional thought. In time, he wished he had.

Lt. Read's Daring Voyage Brought
The Civil War to New England, 1863

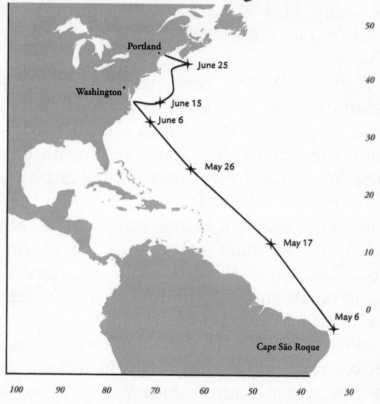

Sources: Captured Confederate Logbooks / Official War Records

Chapter Seven

DANGEROUS MISSION

Off Cape São Roque, Brazil, 5:30 p.m., May 6, 1863

Gentle southeasterly trade winds, hot and laden with equatorial moisture, blew toward the shoulder of Brazil. Cape São Roque marked a bulge in the South American continent that reached farthest into the Atlantic before the shoreline trended west to end in the barren plains of Patagonia and the rocky desolation of Tierra del Fuego more than three thousand miles away. The swells coming in from Africa would soon break on the reefs and beaches at the border of the rain forest and the purple hills beyond. The northeastern reaches of Brazil in 1863 were mostly uninhabited. However, offshore on any given day the sails of merchant vessels from all over the world rose above the horizon. The waters off Cape São Roque represented a major crossroads for shipping bound to and from the Pacific Ocean by way of Cape Horn, and they had recently attracted Confederate commerce destroyers.

With so little wind, the two ships in these waters on May 6 rolled and heaved on an otherwise empty sea, their topsails backed to hold position as boats plied between them. The sails slatted and the running rigging worked in the blocks. At latitude five degrees south in late fall, the sun still dappled the water with sparkles in the waning afternoon. The light's low angle as the sun began its final hours of descent to the west cast shadows from the vessels, and presented welcome shade for the crews sweating at the oars as they came alongside *Florida* for yet another load of ammunition, small arms, and the duffel of the twenty-two sailors selected to board the captured Yankee brig *Clarence*.

At approximately one hundred sixty tons displacement (some sources say she was two hundred fifty tons), *Clarence* was a diminutive vessel, more a coastal trader than a seagoing merchantman. Her hermaphrodite rig consisted of a combination of square sails and fore-and-aft sails, a marriage of a square-rigged ship and a schooner. Such a rig promised a useful versatility in terms of possible sail combinations, though her stubby bowsprit and masts did not allow for setting a broad expanse of canvas. While her lines were not graceful with their pronounced lack of sheer, she looked all business, quite utilitarian. Her dark hull sported a white stripe with false gunports painted at intervals on the bulwarks, giving her the appearance of a gunboat. That type of ornamentation was common in the heyday of the sailing packets plying between New York and Liverpool, now in their twilight of service on the high seas.

Among the men embarking upon the brig was landsman A. L. Drayton. He hurriedly gathered his few belongings and joined the others whom Second Lieutenant Charles W. Read had "volunteered" to serve under his first command as a ship's master. The turn of events since the morning left Drayton confused, surprised, and irritated. Later in the evening, in the dimly lit, smoky forecastle of the brig, he recorded his thoughts in his private journal.

This morning a sail was made from the mast head and after a few hours chase we made her out to be a Brig which we overhauled in fine style and she proved to be the Clarence from Rio de Janeiro to Baltimore [with a cargo of coffee]. We made a prize of her and her Captain and crew were taken on board of the Steamer. Our Prize Crew was just on board for the purpose of searching her and then burning her but for some unknown reason to me Capt. Maffitt changed his mind and put a large crew aboard of her and bound on an unknown expedition. To my great surprise my name was called among the P. C. [prize crew] which was not very agreeable to me as it interrupted my calculations as I intended on arriving at Pernambuco [Brazil] sending a package of letters to England which should have reached home in the course of time. . . .

The work proceeded until six o'clock. Standing on the poop deck of the brig, Read took a long look at *Florida*, her decks crowded with his compatriots, their faces showing evident excitement. Those of the prisoners shackled in chains beside them exhibited the typical look of despair mixed with anger. He turned to Eugene H. Brown, a stoutly built man about Read's age who was to act as first officer during the voyage. As an engineer, Brown was a valuable member of Read's crew. He had served with Read aboard *Arkansas* and was used to leading the men of the black gang, as the firemen, coal heavers, oilers, and mechanics were called, and he possessed the knowledge and skill to operate steam engines. For what Read had in mind, both attributes might prove useful. It did not matter that Brown was in poor health. Read considered himself lucky to have him as an officer.

"We will get underway, Mr. Brown," Read said, his voice stern but quiet, with its slightly feminine tone. He then issued orders Brown was to pass on to the men, in keeping with protocol.

The most experienced seamen among the sailors Read had taken from *Florida* prepared to get underway, and soon they stood ready at the braces and sheets of the square sails. Others were set to trim the sheets of the fore-and-aft sails at the command of their new captain. Like Read, however, they stared across the narrow slot of water separating the two ships, wondering what lay ahead of them. In a few moments, *Clarence*'s sails were drawing and the distance between the vessels widened. The guttural cheers of both crews filled the air. "Huzzah! Huzzah! Huzzah!" they cried. They fell silent at the sound of *Florida*'s propeller churning the sea beneath her transom as she steamed southward toward Pernambuco to resupply and overhaul the engines.

As Drayton watched the steamer depart, he felt both melancholy and curious. "It was like taking a farewell from home to see her go not knowing when we shall see her again and I have no doubt that there are many aboard who think that they have seen the last of us. . . . Speculation is rife among us as what we are going to do. One person told me very confidentially that we were bound to Barbados (all Bosh)." Other rumors included a return to the Confederacy, or the interception of a steamboat known to carry valuable cargo along the coast. As with the first conjecture, Drayton characterized most of the additional guesses as "all gas."

Had Drayton known the true intentions of his new captain, his diary entries might have contained passages showing some alarm. The men of *Clarence* were embarked upon a dangerous, possibly fatal errand. The mission, as originally proposed by Read, had been unrealistically bold and brash. The wisdom of age and experience led Maffitt to draft orders for a less foolhardy attack, though still one with poor odds for success. The official records reveal Read's plan and Maffitt's modification of it.

C. S. Steamer "Florida"
At Sea, May 6, 1863

Sir: I propose to take the brig which we have just captured and with a crew of twenty men to proceed to Hampton Roads and cut out a gunboat or steamer of the enemy.

As I would be in possession of the brig's papers, and as the crew would not be large enough to excite suspicion, there can be no doubt of my passing Fortress Monroe successfully. Once in the Roads, I would be prepared to avail myself of any circumstances which might present for gaining the deck of an enemy's vessel. If it was found impossible to board a gunboat or merchant steamer, it would be possible to fire the shipping at Baltimore.

If you think proper to accede to my proposal, I beg that you will allow me to take Mr. Brown and one of the firemen with me. Mr. Brown might be spared from this ship, as his health is bad, and you could obtain another engineer at Pernambuco.

Very respectfully, your ob't serv't,
C. W. Read,
Second Lieutenant, C.S.N.

Upon reading this letter, Maffitt determined to allow Read to depart with *Clarence*. There is some indication in the record, though not definite, that Maffitt may have been glad to be rid of Read and that the young man's proposal gave him a perfect opportunity to send him on a voyage that would get him off *Florida* and, if successful, prove injurious to the enemy, thereby accomplishing two happy objectives. Evidently, Maffitt had suggested on an earlier occasion to Read that *Florida* might head to the Far East to attack American shipping. In response, Read threatened to resign his commission, return to the Confederacy, and join the Army, saying that such a move was not the best use of the cruiser. The petulance of the youthful outburst, if it occurred, was not new to Maffitt in dealing with his junior officers. He confided his observations to his journal on April 15, while coaling from *Lapwing*, a Yankee trader captured on March 28 off the Azores and converted to a commerce raider, though not a very successful one.

I have always observed that coaling is demoralizing to a ship's company. The dirt and temporary abnegation of the usual formality of a man-of-war produces a general laxity that cannot be avoided unless the officers are experienced in proper discipline of naval jurisprudence. Unfortunately, the young officers of this vessel lack that training. I have good reason to regret their want of vim and early training, that would no doubt have made them more observant, careful, and military. They would in battle fight well, but do not seem fully to appreciate the training that is necessary for the purpose of being formidable when the trial comes. Too vapid.

Above all else, Maffitt was a veteran seaman and an experienced naval officer savvy enough to note and try to correct the deficiencies of his men. Whether it pleased him for personal reasons to send Read on what amounted to an impossible mission remains an open question. His official answer to Read suggests no animosity, nor would it likely have done so if any existed between them. It nevertheless confined him to attacks in the vicinity of Hampton Roads, not Baltimore, and offered advice on how to escape back to Confederate lines after the assault.

C.S. Steamer "Florida,"
At Sea, May 6, 1863

Sir: Your proposition of this date has been duly considered, — under such advisement as the gravity of the case demands. The conclusion reached is that you may meet with success by centering your views upon Hampton Roads. The Sumpter (a Cromwell steamer) is now a kind of flag-ship anchored off Hampton Bar, and at midnight might be carried by boarding. If you find that impractical, the large quantity of shipping at the Fort, or in Norfolk, could be fired and you and your crew escape to Burrell's Bay, thence making your way in safety to the Confederate lines.

The proposition evinces on your part patriotic devotion to the cause of your country, and this is certainly the time when all our best exertions should be made to harm the common enemy and confuse them with attacks from all unexpected quarters. I agree to your request and will not hamper you with instructions.

Act for the best, and God-speed you. If success attends the effort, you will deserve the fullest consideration of the Department, and it will be my pleasure to urge a just recognition of the same.

Under all circumstances, you will receive from me the fullest justice for the intent and public spirit that influences the proposal.

I give you a howitzer and ammunition, that you may have the means of capture if an opportunity offers *en route*.

Wishing you success and a full reward for
the same,
I am, yours very truly,
J. N. Maffitt, C.S.N.
Lieut., Comdg. C. S. S. *Florida*

Read's proposition demonstrated his ambition to hit the Union hard in its own waters, a desire that increased in urgency since he had served as executive officer aboard *McRea*, when the idea first occurred to him. It burgeoned to grandiose proportions, fed by the heat of his patriotism and a want for personal glory and promotion. Now, the wish transformed to opportunity, and he relished the moment as *Clarence* made her way slowly through the tropical seas. *Florida* disappeared astern in the gathering twilight, her presence made known from the occasional spray of red embers exiting her two funnels.

With luck, his foray into the largest depot of the U.S. Navy would succeed. Maffitt stated that he intended to steam north as well. They agreed that if it were possible for Read to escape capture after his raid in Hampton Roads, and a viable chance presented itself, instead of turning back for Burrell's Bay and the Confederate lines beyond, he should cruise northward to a rendezvous with *Florida* off Nantucket on or around June 20. They would form a tiny squadron with the objective of destroying Yankee merchantmen in a stretch of ocean far busier than the waters off Cape São Roque.

Read organized the men into starboard and port watches and allowed them all to "splice the main brace," a sailor's term for drinking. As the men gathered on deck to enjoy their grog, with great flair and pomp Read renamed the brig *Florida No. 2*. While not very creative, the new name was in keeping with the custom. Subsequent to converting *Lapwing* into a raider, Maffitt rechristened her *Oreto*. Read followed his mentor's example. He also appointed three of the men to act as petty officers. Brown was to serve as executive officer.

Soon after leaving *Florida*, the junior officers took stock of the provisions on board. They had brought none of consequence from the steamer. In fact, the initial boarding party stripped the brig of everything useful or valuable. This included all the pots and pans from the galley, leaving the cook to use tin pails and whatever other containers he might find as he tried to feed the crew. A thorough search of the brig turned up two barrels of half-rotten salt pork, which sailors the world over termed *old horse* even when in good condition, because it was usually tough and foul tasting. In addition, there were two barrels of flour, one of bread, and a large tank of water. The present number of men aboard greatly exceeded those of the crew taken prisoner. It was 3,400 miles to Chesapeake Bay from their current position, and that on a straight-line course. The provisions would not last the duration of the voyage. Read did not tell the men. In time, the situation would become obvious to them all.

The morning of May 7 dawned bright, hot, and nearly calm, with *Clarence* "going along as quiet as a lamb," in Drayton's words. Stripped to their pantaloons and covered in sweat, the sailors worked in the stuffy, fetid bowels of the ship to restore order in the hold after the previous day's ransacking. It was vital to make the brig look the part of a Yankee in case a boarding crew from a Union cruiser snooped about. If that occurred, the men would dress in clothing left behind by the Union sailors. Not all of them spoke with heavy Southern accents; the ruse might work. However, no one aboard *Clarence* wanted to put it to the test.

In a seeming contradiction to adopting the role of the harmless merchantman, the following day, under Read's orders, the crew set to work cutting and sculpting spare spars into the shape of cannons. They were called *Quaker guns*. From a distance, they would look real enough. With only a small howitzer, more a signal gun than a serious weapon, *Clarence* needed an imposing gun battery to become a commerce destroyer. The crew also built a raised walkway on the poop deck for Read. Its purpose was to enhance his view of the horizon. He made the bridge his territory and walked back and forth across the width of the ship like a caged tiger, aloof and silent, lost in thoughts he did not share.

The fair weather off the coast of Brazil gave way to the rain and squalls of the doldrums after *Clarence* crossed the equator and continued sailing north-northwest.

She lost the weak southeasterly trades and entered the belt of calms that spanned the Atlantic Ocean from Africa to South America, and marked a zone of misery for sailors. The brig rolled to the swells, her sails flaccid, the timbers of her hull creaking and groaning as they worked. The crew watched the sky darken with each approaching squall, and anticipated the chaos that would soon arrive. The experienced seamen expected to scurry aloft to shorten canvas, but the orders to reef never came. Similarly, the landlubbers aboard wondered about the captain's lack of caution and the reasons for it.

". . . We have carried Top Gallant Studding Sails [through the squalls] and if others had control light sails would have been taken in but the Florida's usual good luck attends us for it is more by good luck than good management that she has fared as well as she has," Drayton wrote.

The first hot breaths of the storm whipped the surface of the ocean into short, steep waves, and a wall of rain rushed toward the ship sounding like a waterfall. The flash of nearly continuous lightning and the roar of thunder accompanied the rising wind. The brig buried her lee rail, staggered under her press of sail, and cut through the waves at her best speed, only to slow and finally stop again when the squall passed. Some storms brought little or no wind. At each opportunity, as the rain drummed on the deck and *Clarence* drifted on a flat sea, the crew caught water running off spare sails and filled empty casks. Upon drinking it, all were disappointed. The water was foul with the taste of paint and tar.

By May 17, *Clarence* had sailed clear of the doldrums. She picked up the Northeast trades, which blow from a more easterly quarter in those waters at that time of year. They provided a favorable slant for sailing with the breeze off the beam. Read, who remained in his cabin away from the crew and his petty officers most of the time, emerged from below with his sextant in hand. With an assistant to mark the ship's local time upon his orders, he took his morning sights. At around noon, when the sun reached its highest point in the sky, he got the celestial measurements needed to determine his latitude.

Although a poor student at the Naval Academy, he possessed the necessary skills to navigate proficiently — a natural knack for mathematics that surfaced in his training as a gunner. Figuring range and trajectory of ordnance, and adjusting the elevation of the gun to account for it, made sense to him even if his grades were just above passing. The array of figures and calculations needed to determine a ship's position using celestial navigation likewise came easily.

His work with the sextant done, Read returned to his cabin to work out the brig's position, scarcely saying a word to his junior officers. He stared at the chart, his face grim. Rivulets of sweat ran down his well-tanned cheeks and dripped from his goatee onto the papers spread out on the desk. Based on his noon sight, *Clarence* cruised 900 miles east of Barbados and 600 miles north of Cabo Norte at the entrance to the vast Amazon River Basin. She had made good approximately one thousand two hundred miles since May 6. In spite of his efforts to drive the brig hard and his sound reasons for haste, he failed to get her to make much better than one hundred miles per day. At this rate, it might take close to another month to reach Chesapeake Bay. Without capturing a Yankee ship or help from a neutral vessel sympathetic to the Confederacy, their food and water would be gone before then.

Clarence sailed on, far from the crowded

shipping lanes near the islands of the eastern Caribbean, and thus reduced the odds of encountering a Union warship. As the days passed and rationing began, the brig lumbered into the calm Sargasso Sea, known for its fickle winds and baffling currents. It appeared to the crew as if they were to cruise forever into oblivion on this unknown expedition under the command of a taciturn young officer whom they were compelled out of circumstance to entrust with their lives, an officer with a secret he refused to divulge. The crew's discontentment increased until it pervaded the ship and threatened to explode into violence.

Chapter Eight

TROPICAL FIRE

Pernambuco, Brazil, May 20, 1863

The endless South Atlantic swell crashed with stupendous force against the long, uniform band of sandstone fronting the large city of Pernambuco, as it had well before people settled the fringe of the interior hinterlands in northeastern Brazil. The roar of the surf became louder at low tide, when the top of the reef protecting the inner harbor dried out and the waves hit precipitous rock. Yellowish brown spray laden with sediment flew upward from the ocean side of the reef and the southeasterly trade winds carried it over the top. At high tide, the seas rolled across the craggy formation and tossed the small boats tied to the wooden wharves along the waterfront. Large ships, anchored behind this natural breakwater, tugged at their cables and rode still only when the tide was fully out.

153

Pernambuco (present-day Recife) was built on sand banks collected in a bight of lowlands cradled by a half-circle of forested hills rising 200 feet above the town. Swamps and stands of mangrove bordered it, and bred yellow fever and other diseases deadly to natives and foreigners alike. Charles Darwin had visited there in 1836, near the end of his long voyage aboard HMS *Beagle*. Although the city had grown in subsequent decades, it retained its inhospitable character. Darwin described Pernambuco in his journal.

Pernambuco is built on some narrow and low sand-banks, which are separated from each other by shoal channels of salt water. The three parts of the town are connected together by two long bridges built on wooden piles. The town is in all parts disgusting, the streets being narrow, ill-paved, and filthy; the houses, tall and gloomy. . . . [The mangroves] always reminded me of the rank grass in a churchyard; both are nourished by putrid exhalations; the one speaks of death past, and the other too often of death to come.

The port city was by no means a major

harbor, nothing like Bahia or Rio de Janeiro. However, it was conveniently close to Cape São Roque. When the winds blew foul and retarded the progress of sailing vessels bound to Africa or Europe, it became a haven of sorts, a refuge from the turbulent sea in spite of its hygienic deficiencies. The Brazilian government welcomed all comers, and this welcome included any ships that cared to call from the Union or the Confederacy. Like the British, Brazil favored the South. Living in a country with a long tradition of slavery, Brazil's wealthy class closely identified with the Confederate struggle to maintain an institution upon which the longevity of its economy depended.

The violence and depravity of slavery resonated with Darwin when he visited Brazil. Where slavery existed, most ordinary British subjects found it abhorrent, whether in Brazil, the United States, or elsewhere. That the British government and business community largely supported the South for political and economic reasons represented a paradox not lost on individuals perceptive enough to take it into account. The slaves in Brazil would have to wait until 1888 for freedom. Darwin's journal mentioned in detail the conditions slaves endured at the hands of their Brazilian owners. They were much the same in the Confederacy.

I thank God, I shall never again visit a slave country. To this day, if I hear a distant scream, it recalls with painful vividness my feelings, when passing a house near Pernambuco, I heard the most pitiable moans, and could not but suspect that some poor slave was being tortured, yet knew that I was as powerless as a child to even remonstrate. . . .

Near Rio de Janeiro I lived opposite to an old lady, who kept screws to crush the fingers of her female slaves. I have stayed in a house where a young household mulatto, daily and hourly, was reviled, beaten, and persecuted enough to break the spirit of the lowest animal. . . . I have seen at Rio de Janeiro a powerful negro afraid to ward off a blow directed, as he thought, at his face. I was present when a kind-hearted man was on the point of separating for ever the men, women, and little children of a large number of families who had long lived together.

I will not even allude to the many heart-sickening atrocities which I authentically heard of: — nor would I have mentioned the above revolting details, had I not met with several people, so blinded by the constitutional gaiety of the negro, as to speak of slavery as a tolerable evil. . . .

In addition, like the British, many Brazilian officials walked a tightrope of international law and tried to appear neutral while supporting their Confederate brethren. In recent days, that delicate balance had been upset. The commandant of Fernando de Noronha, a group of islands situated approximately 240 miles north-northeast of Pernambuco, allowed Raphael Semmes to overstep the legal bounds governing the behavior of belligerents in neutral territory. For a short time, and with the official's blessings, *Alabama* conducted sorties from the anchorage, burning two American ships within sight of the islands before steaming back to the port. The Brazilians recalled the commandant as a gesture designed to appease the American Consul, but the sentiments were clear: Rebel commerce destroyers were free to come and go as they pleased. In Pernambuco, the Americans protested against the overcourteous treatment of *Florida*, which had called there on May 8 and stayed until May 12, three days longer than she should have under the terms of international law, with the sanction and approval of the province's president.

Captain O. S. Glisson, commander of the cruiser USS *Mohican*, was all too aware of the presence of the raiders. They were close. Tantalizingly close. And he was determined to capture or sink them. Word of their whereabouts had reached him 1,500 miles away at Porto Grande in the Cape Verde Islands off the coast of Africa on May 9, when a French mail steamer arrived there with the latest news of destruction. He got his ship underway immediately and steamed full ahead to Pernambuco, arriving on May 20, missing *Florida* by eight days. With all possible speed, he set his officers to work supervising the recoaling of the ship's bunkers, and went ashore to learn more about his quarry. He discovered information so important that he collected the data and sent it directly to Gideon Welles the afternoon he made port. In part, his communiqués noted the destruction of ten American vessels in Brazilian waters within the last month.

Through the night of May 20, the crew of *Mohican* toiled in the tropical heat. Coal dust hung in the air. The forms of men blackened to the skin from the coal moved briskly about on deck. Their captain insisted on leaving the following day, and he made it clear that no one was allowed to slack off. The following afternoon, all the work done, and the ship ready to sail, Glisson sent yet another dispatch to Welles. In it he wrote: "A vessel has this moment arrived from Bahia and informed me that the Alabama and Virginia [*Georgia*] has sailed from that port to join the *Florida* at sea, and that in future they will sail in squadron, so the honorable Secretary will see the importance of having more vessels on this coast." The letter was sent ashore to the U.S. Consul, and *Mohican* set sail, her master convinced that it would not be long before a battle occurred.

It took weeks for the information to reach Welles. When it did, he learned that the rebel threat on the high seas had dramatically increased. He knew of CSS *Georgia*, an iron vessel of 600 tons faster than all but *Vanderbilt*. British-built and identified as a merchantman, she sailed from England on April 1 under the name of *Virginia* and was rechristened CSS *Georgia* on April 9. American agents rightly thought she was intended for use as a Confederate raider, but like her sisters she disappeared into the broad Atlantic. Now he knew where she was.

Glisson's dispatches also contained interesting information about two additional raiders, prizes converted to instruments of war — *Lapwing* and *Clarence*. He scrawled a note on Glisson's letter of May 21 and handed it to a clerk: "Write to him to follow them anywhere. Must send other vessels, though *Vanderbilt* is, I think, on her way there by this."

Like a malignancy spreading through a host, the commerce destroyers multiplied, slowly dividing and doubling with frightening vigor. One of them drew closer to the United States with each passing day.

Chapter Nine

Well-Guarded Secret

Sargasso Sea, 300 Miles North of St. Martin, May 26, 1863

Clarence rode nearly still on a placid ocean tinged a peculiar deep blue that experienced sailors recognized as a hallmark of the Sargasso Sea. To the west, the Gulf Stream flowed up the coast of the United States and trended eastward, gradually weakening as it reached England, France, and Scandinavia. Off Africa, the Canary Current set southward, and eventually branched into the North Equatorial Current streaming west. The currents formed a giant ring of clockwise moving water and at its center was the Sargasso Sea, a portion of the Atlantic more than two million square miles in area. Aboard *Clarence*, as she lay becalmed at its southern edge at latitude 24 degrees north, it seemed to the men that the brig was caught in a sort of netherworld, where a ship might remain trapped indefinitely.

No clouds passed overhead. The few intermittent puffs of wind lacked the strength to even ruffle the sails hanging limp from the yards. Patches of weed held suspended just beneath the surface with thousands of tiny air sacs stretched out for miles on either side of the brig. The unusual clarity of the sea allowed light to penetrate over a half mile down, and it gave one the impression of peering into a body every bit as grand as the heavens spangled with the twinkling pricks of countless stars.

The sound of loud voices carried over the otherwise quiet waters. The men argued frequently, and on this day the conflict arose over the universal objection to going into the galley to cook. The man assigned to the task endured great abuse, objected to it, and refused to prepare dinner. Such conduct would never have been tolerated on a ship of the United States Navy, but according to Drayton lapses of discipline and overindulgence in alcoholic beverages were a matter of routine. Read, in his reclusive ways, left the day-to-day operations of managing the vessel to his subordinates. They executed their duties with an excess of inflated ego that translated into an overbearing demeanor. Drayton described them as "apes" and of Lieutenant Read he wrote:

> Mr. R is not the Capt. for all we see of him is when he is taking the Sun: he never gives orders never has any thing to say to any one: awfully reserved. I do not think it is an empty pride that influences him but more likely disgust for his associates. Wonder where the Devil we are bound to. The secret is well kept, can't get at it no how.

It was common enough for a crewman to find his superiors lacking in many respects. Deriding officers constituted a form of entertainment among sailors before the mast in both merchantmen and warships. Adding the mystery of the cruise and Read's eccentric behavior to the typical mix of shipboard irritations exacerbated the usual state of affairs.

Aft in his small private cabin below the poop deck, Read viewed the situation from a much different perspective. Discipline problems were to be expected. There were occasions aboard *Florida* when similar events occurred, events that Maffitt found quite out of keeping with the tradition of the U.S. Navy but of necessity accepted in the fledgling navy of his newly formed country. Maffitt pursued a compromise between laxity and overzealous enforcement of the rules, which would alienate the men instead of forming them into a tight fighting unit. Foreseeing the action to come, Read adopted a similar mode of command, and allowed the grog to flow more than it should have and the arguments among the men to work themselves out without interference from him or his officers.

Apart from Maffitt's example to lead with a strong hand while granting leeway for petty squabbles on board ship, Read's style of leadership stemmed from his aloof and independent nature. He had from an early age made his own decisions and fought his own battles without seeking redress from a higher authority. In fact, he had bucked authority all his life. His mother, Maria, found him a difficult boy to raise. When he was a child growing up on the farm his parents struggled to maintain even as their debts increased, Read, the eldest of his brothers and sister — John, Joseph, Elizabeth, and William — found the life dull and oppressive. Working in the fields with his father, William, and his brothers, offered little of the intellectual stimulation or the excitement he craved. He longed for something better, though he did not know what.

When the Gold Rush fever swept through the nation in 1849, Read's father left the family to fend for itself and headed to California. Read's grandfather, John, a staunch Union man and veteran of the War of 1812, lived nearby and watched over the family as much as possible. Nevertheless, Read found himself the man of the house at the age of nine. It would have been natural for him, as well as the rest of the family, to feel a sense of abandonment and desolation. Read's father never returned to Mississippi. He died on July 6, 1850, in Nevada City, California.

Read's tenth year was even more trying. Deep in debt and devoid of all hope for making the farm viable enough to support the family, Maria sold it and moved the children to Jackson, the bustling capital of Mississippi. She had relatives and some powerful friends in Jackson, and felt the future might hold brighter prospects for her sons and daughter in the big city. For a time, it seemed Maria was right. Read appeared to adjust well to a more urban existence. He occupied himself in writing for local newspapers in his early teens, including *The Mississippian*, an accomplishment that revealed keen intelligence and ability with language, though his prose was still quite raw. He also joined a theater group and polished his talents as an actor.

Yet Read was never really fully at ease with himself or his surroundings, regardless of the promise he showed. He stirred up trouble with some of his newspaper writings, and eventually ran away to New Orleans, where he signed on as a crewman aboard a merchant ship. His mother did not envision her son as a virtual slave before the mast, a sailor whose future would likely end in death at sea or in poverty in his old age. She managed to void the contract Read had signed with the captain and bring her son home to Jackson. Realizing Read needed discipline and a more structured environment, Maria successfully lobbied influential members of Mississippi's political elite to recommend Read for an appointment to the U.S. Naval Academy. He passed his entrance exams and reported for his four-year stint as a cadet in July 1856.

Read may not have been a good student in Annapolis, but he found in the navy a sense of belonging and a chance to play a part in something bigger than an individual making his own way in the world. The system of rules and regulations he could live with. Authority had its place in an organization such as the navy. Its function was essential to the continuation of the long tradition. His most productive time at the Naval Academy was aboard the training ship *Plymouth* in 1859, as he applied the classroom lessons of seamanship, navigation, and gunnery to the actual experience of operating a ship under sail on the wide ocean, calling at ports in far-off places such as France and Spain.

The U.S. Navy was a home for Read, an institution that grounded him more than at any other time in his life. However, he was not inclined to stay within its ranks when Mississippi seceded from the Union in January 1861 while he was stationed aboard the cruiser *Powhatan* off Vera Cruz in the Gulf of Mexico. Against his grandfather's wishes, and, in fact, in direct defiance of the old veteran, Read resigned his commission to join the rebel cause. He would find a new path, just as the newly formed Confederate States of America would, and it might present opportunities for greatness. Now, two years into the war and with the

South marching triumphantly to victory on many fronts, Read had realized some of the ambitions that had taken root long ago. He was determined to give the mission at hand every chance for success, and that required him to accomplish exactly what Maffitt was able to do aboard *Florida*: form an effective unit of fighters from a loose band of diverse personalities.

Toward that end, as *Clarence* sailed slowly northwest across the Sargasso Sea, Read set the men to gunnery practice with the wooden cannons they had labored so hard to build. The crew at first found it amusing to pretend to load, then actually run the guns out of the ports cut in the bulwarks. They stood at attention near the guns, with fake firing lanyards in hand. In the heat of the tropics, the amusement did not last long. Read also drilled the men in live fire exercises with the pistols comprising the bulk of the small arms requisitioned from *Florida*. Very few of the sailors aboard *Clarence* knew how to shoot a pistol. They lined up in ranks and shot at a target propped against the anchor secured forward on the forecastle deck while the brig sailed well offshore. Their first drill gave all aboard a bit of welcome excitement — too much for one man who might

168

have been seriously injured or killed.

Orders were given to discharge the pistols . . . one of the balls glanced from the anchor over the forecastle companion way striking Robinson in the shoulder inflicting a bruise; fortunately for him that was not his eye, if it had been I have no doubt but that he would have lost his sight. It certainly was foolish to put the target there at all as some of them could not hit a barn door. M. hit the target twice and sent his other shots through the foresail. Wonder what he was shooting at.

The target practice and gunnery drills helped break up the monotony of the voyage. As *Clarence* made her way past the islands of the eastern Caribbean and entered busier waters, the sight of sails on the horizon became a more frequent occurrence. Two days past, on May 24, the lookout reported a sail off the weather bow at 9:00 a.m. The men watched her anxiously as they went about their duties and wondered if she was *Florida*. They now thought the reason for the cruise was to meet *Florida*, and possibly *Alabama*, to attack shipping in northern waters. This time the rumors were more accurate, though none of the men except Read knew it. At the turn of the watches at noon it appeared that the vessel was on an intercepting course, and the excitement on board became intense. Read emerged from his lair below the poop deck. Strutting to and fro on his little bridge, he studied the vessel through the lens of his glass. The two ships drew nearer and the rebel cruiser ran up the Stars and Stripes, her gun crew at the ready with the one real cannon aboard.

Read quietly called out orders to the helmsman and relayed others to the crewmen at their sail stations through First Officer Brown. The chase was a British bark sailing along without changing course, her master confident that a United States vessel would not likely bother her in open waters far from any blockaded port. She hove to, however, after *Clarence* fired a warning shot. Her captain agreed to trade some provisions for coffee, the Confederates posing as Yankee privateers short on rations. Read intended to keep his mission secret, and believed that one way to do so was to conceal the true character of his vessel even from a ship full of Confederate supporters. Sailors ashore talked too much when drunk in the taverns. Word might get out to Union spies or officials that a raider was seen far to the north, and gunboats would no doubt begin searching for the brig. "We told them that we were Yankee Privateers, but if the Capt. believed it the crew did not . . . our boys said nothing [to give themselves away]."

Read promptly divided the provisions obtained from the British merchantman among all the crew. Their spirits rose. Later in the afternoon, *Clarence* overhauled another British ship and forced her to heave to, this time without firing a shot. The sailors standing ready at the Quaker guns looked frightening. Again pretending to be American privateers, *Clarence*'s crew bartered coffee for additional provisions.

The Yankee newspapers received from the Britisher were passed to members of the crew who could read, and the men who were illiterate listened to the news read out loud. Drayton was one of the more educated of the lot. Indeed, he was a man of means, with land holdings along the Brazos River in Texas, replete with vineyards and fig trees. He had joined *Florida* in Mobile Bay out of a sense of patriotism he came to regret. Before signing on his father called him a fool, insisting that a landsman playing at being a sailor on a commerce destroyer was bound to disappoint and frustrate him in spite of his hankering to fight for the Confederacy.

"I wish that something had turned to cool my enthusiasm [for joining *Florida*], breaking an arm or something else that would have compelled me to have gone home," Drayton wrote on May 21. The following day he felt no less homesick, or more to the point, no less an urge to return to land as long as he was away from the sea: "Oh for a cot in some vast wilderness or rather my own comfortable home on the Brazos."

Drayton spent hours while off watch reading the newspapers from cover to cover. Reading provided an escape from the dull apathy that assailed him, an escape from the unhappy voyage he found himself forced to undertake upon departing *Florida*. Like the rest of the men's, his morale improved, though it was only a temporary respite. The monotony closed in again and the discontentment, never really banished, descended like a bank of wind-driven clouds obliterating the sun.

Thus, on May 26, with more than 1,100 miles still to go before *Clarence* reached the mouth of Chesapeake Bay, the brig resembled more a hell ship than a Confederate commerce destroyer, her Stars and Bars flying proudly from the peak of her mizzen gaff. It remained so the next day, and the next, as the weather turned foul, bringing rain, squalls, and light winds of sufficient velocity to creep the brig toward her objective. While the barter for food staved off the possibility of their starving at sea, water remained scarce. The sailors availed themselves of every opportunity to catch the rain and channel it into empty casks. Some of them washed their clothes and bathed in the downpours; others did not. The paucity of water worried everyone, despite occasional replenishment when it rained. Rationing began once more.

Clarence slowly ticked off the miles on a north-northwesterly course, chasing and failing to catch a couple of Union merchantmen because of, in Read's words expressed in his official report, her "inferior sailing qualities." Several weeks later, a letter from the captain of one of the vessels Read chased served as the basis for a report in the New-Haven Journal. The brief account confirmed the slow sailing abilities of *Clarence*, a fact that led Read to make an important decision. It also demonstrated the courage of the Yankee captain.

Capt. N. E. Perkins, of the brig *George*,

of this port, in a private letter dated St. Croix, June 2, writes, that, on Tuesday evening on May 28, in lat. 25.30. lon. 64, his vessel was chased by a hermaphrodite brig, which gained upon him slowly. When within half a mile of the *George*, the pirate fired his bow gun twice, and, after following about an hour, he fired three guns more, the last ball passing to windward of the *George*, about twenty feet off, as near as Capt. Perkins could judge. The *George* kept on her course, and three days afterward went safely into St. Croix, where she was bound. Capt. Perkins is a plucky seaman, and deserves credit for not coming to and giving himself up, as many captains would have done under the circumstances. The underwriters ought to remember him.

Drayton mentioned this ship in his diary on May 28, though not by name. He said they all "admired the [master's] spunk" and wished the wind might drop off, allowing them to send an armed boat crew to board her at gunpoint. In that eventuality, Drayton wrote, warming to the thought, "he is a gone Yank."

The weather cooled off as the brig

passed out of tropical waters into the more temperate climate off the coast of the Carolinas. The men snuggled under blankets in their hammocks at night. By day, Read kept the ship on her usual course, but come evening he put her on an offshore tack, heading eastward out into the Atlantic and fooling some of the sailors into thinking they were bound for Liverpool. Soon, they all fully realized the danger of their position when Read ordered the men to make sure turpentine, sperm whale oil, lard, and tallow along with flammable materials — tar, rags, wood shavings, and the like — were ready in case they were forced to burn the brig. He also prepared to jettison the Quaker guns if a Union cruiser approached too near. Bermuda lay just to the northeast about 450 miles away. Yankee warships regularly patrolled these waters hoping to catch blockade runners. *Clarence*'s lookouts saw many vessels, in contrast to the weeks spent farther south when nothing but empty horizon surrounded the brig. On some days, they counted more than a dozen sail.

"We are now in the track of the Yankee cruisers and if we should not be smart enough to deceive them they will not derive much benefit from our capture as we intend to fire her if we find out that they are going to seize the vessel. If we do they will certainly treat us fairly roughly but d—d the odds it will be some satisfaction to know that we prevent them from making a recapture," Drayton wrote on June 1.

Five days later, *Clarence* arrived at the same latitude *Florida* reached on February 6, while fighting to her farthest point north in the grip of a rare winter cyclone. The storm had turned the steamer back from the home waters of the Union, but there was little chance of that happening to *Clarence*. Fair winds at last sent the brig onward. She cut through the swells, a flash of white at her bow, the rigging stretched taut. Although a slow sailer, she appeared beautiful in her element as she advanced steadily toward the Yankee coast.

Lt. Read's 21 Attacks on US Merchant Vessels Between June 6 and June 24, 1863

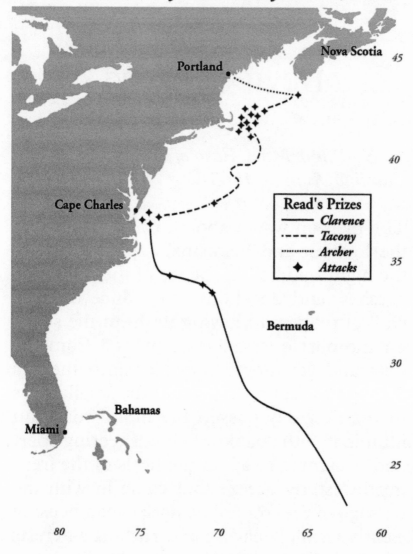

Source: Official War Records

Chapter Ten

DEVIL'S CARTEL

At Sea, 360 Miles East of Cape Fear, North Carolina, June 6, 1863

The men on watch aboard *Clarence*, all save the lookout and helmsman, spent much of the night huddled in the lee of the bulwarks, hatches, and deckhouse to reduce the raw chill of the wind blowing up from the south off the port quarter. Rain poured from the sails and ran down the deck into the sea through the scuppers. But as the small hours of the new day passed the moon rose and illuminated the banks of clouds tearing apart and streaming away on the heels of the fresh northwesterly breeze that came in with the passage of the front. The dark ocean became clearly visible, heaving and rushing in crests of white flecked green from the fireflylike glow of phosphorescence. Close-hauled, with the yards braced sharply forward and fore-and-aft sails sheeted tight, the brig kept her course toward land, the captain having changed his routine of standing offshore at sunset.

Dawn brought the now familiar shout from aloft, "Sail ho! Broad on the lee bow."

Read emerged from his cabin and took his post on the bridge. He studied the vessel, concluding that she was a Yankee brig. In a lack of action inexplicable to his men, he gave no orders to intercept her, though it would have been easy. He remained at his customary roost on the windward side of the ship and scanned the horizon with his glass. Two more sails appeared in the strengthening light. A schooner made way under full sail off the port bow. Of more interest to Read, a bark flying the flag of his enemy hove into view dead ahead. He watched her for a while, then called to his first officer to muster all hands on deck to tack the ship.

The sailors off-watch tumbled to and together with their companions on watch hauled the braces to turn the yards supporting the square sails for the new course. They pulled hard on the lines as the brig's head swung through the eye of the wind and the canvas thundered and shook.

Their hands were rough and callused from the nearly five straight months at sea that had tanned their skin deep brown in the tropical sun. Most of them wore thick, untrimmed beards, and their hair, matted from salt, sweat, and dirt, had grown long enough to reach their shoulders. Four of the men wore colorful shirts cut and sewn from the tablecloths taken from the clipper ship *Jacob Bell*, and they made a fancy sight next to the more plainly clad members of the crew. Not many wore the uniform of the Confederate Navy; uniforms were a luxury in scarce supply.

Clarence heeled to the wind, beating to weather at all possible speed with the United States flag conspicuous at the peak of the mizzen gaff. The confused seas kicked up from the shift in the wind broke against her bow and sent spray flying aft over the forecastle deck, drenching the men at the little howitzer, ready to fire. The entire crew watched with anticipation to see whether the brig might at last give them a Yankee prize, but the excitement soon diminished. The American vessel sailed better than *Clarence*. That was no surprise to any of them, yet was still disappointing. She slowly drew away.

"Half-mast the colors," Read said, and

ordered the men forward to cover up the howitzer and those stationed at the Quaker guns to run them back in.

The officer of the deck followed Read's instructions and relayed the order to lower the colors and belay the guns. A disciplined commotion ensued as the crew obeyed. The wooden cannons were dragged inboard, the ports closed. Gunners at the bow covered the howitzer with a canvas tarpaulin. A sailor hauled the flag from the peak, turned it upside down, and raised it halfway up the length of its halyard. This was an internationally recognized distress signal. The brig looked harmless, just another of the many ships in the area in need of help from a friend. It was the duty of a ship's captain to render aid to another vessel requiring assistance, a tenet of the sea centuries old that did not account for the deceptions of war. The rebels turned this to their advantage.

Drayton glanced from the bark back to the pages of his diary, scribbling a terse record of the events at the moment they occurred: "While I am writing the word has come that he is bearing down for us. We have got him!"

Captain Butler of the bark *Whistling Wind* ordered his men to heave to a safe distance from the brig without the least hint of suspicion that he had been fooled. He was well within the patrol area of Union cruisers and far from the supposed location of any Confederate commerce destroyers. The three known to exist — *Florida*, *Alabama*, and *Georgia* — steamed thousands of miles away off the coast of Brazil, or in the eastern Caribbean. Continued news of their depredations reminded masters sailing in those waters that caution must prevail. Bound from Philadelphia for New Orleans with a cargo of 450 tons of anthracite coal for the Union Navy, he believed any chance of meeting a raider would not occur until he sailed much farther south, and at that the odds for trouble were slim. He watched as a boat filled with men dressed in clothing typical of a merchantman's crew made its way to the side of the bark. The sailors climbed a Jacob's ladder hung against the hull to enable them to board easily. The man evidently in charge strode aft to the poop deck.

"Good day, sir," the stranger said. "Where do you hail from and where are you bound?"

Butler told him. "What is the nature of your distress?" Butler asked.

"We are of the brig *Clarence*, bound from

Rio de Janeiro for Baltimore. We are short of water and provisions."

Butler nodded and ordered his first officer to break out a barrel of flour, all he could spare, since he was at the start of his voyage and needed to take care not to run short of supplies himself. His men began removing the battens from the main hatch while others rigged block and tackle to hoist the barrel from the hold.

"Have you any arms aboard?" the stranger asked.

"No, sir. I don't," Butler said.

The question must have perplexed Butler, but before he could think much of it the man standing in front of him drew a pistol and pointed it directly at his forehead. At the same time, the rest of the boarders pulled guns on the crew.

"You are a prize of the Confederate States of America!"

Butler stared at the rebel, momentarily speechless, then quietly said, "All right."

Within a few minutes, his crew of six men, two of whom were black and quite upset about finding themselves in rebel hands, two mates, the steward, and the supercargo were all on deck lined up against the lee bulwarks staring at the guns. Although the black crewmen did not know it, they were in no danger. They had not taken up arms against the South, unlike black soldiers in the Union Army, who would sometimes be murdered after surrendering. They were viewed as private property not subject to destruction under the terms of international law, unlike the ship and her cargo. Both definitely could be legally destroyed as commercial property of the United States, either owned by its citizens or its government; it did not matter which.

"Tell your men not to resist us," the rebel officer said. The threat of murder remained unspoken.

The two ships lay hove to for the rest of the day while Read and his men took what they wanted and transferred the goods to *Clarence*. As was the custom, they allowed each crewman of the Union bark, including the blacks, to pack one small bag of clothing and any personal belongings that would fit inside. Once aboard, these bags were searched for guns, knives, razors, and matches, lest the prisoners attempt to recapture or burn the brig. The boarding crew set fire to *Whistling Wind* as dusk fell. It was a sight both beautiful and awful. The Yankee mariners would long replay the moment in their memories.

Perhaps the best description of "firing" a sailing ship came from Raphael Semmes. It is a passage only an eyewitness could write, and it is one an arsonist might admire:

The prize ship had been laid to with her main-topsail to the mast, and all her light sails, though clewed up, were flying loose about the yards. The forked tongues of the devouring element, leaping into the rigging, newly tarred, ran rapidly up the shrouds, first into the tops, then to the topmastheads, thence to the top-gallant, and royal mastheads, and in a moment more to the trucks; and whilst this rapid ascent of the main current of fire was going on, other currents had run out upon the yards and ignited all the sails. . . .

At one time, the intricate network of the cordage of the burning ship was traced as with a pencil of fire upon the black sky beyond, the many threads of flame twisting and writhing like so many serpents that had received their death wounds. The mizzen-mast now went by the board, then the foremast, and in a few minutes afterward, the great mainmast tottered, reeled, and fell over the ship's side into the sea, making a noise like that of the sturdy oak of the forests when it falls by the stroke of the axeman.

The flames enveloping *Whistling Wind* created a beacon that might lure other ships into a trap, their masters intent upon effecting a rescue, only to become victims themselves. It was a common trick among raiders and was very effective at drawing vessels within range of their guns, which was why they often burned their prizes at night. Read was aware of the tactic, but he was also aware that the burning wreck might attract a Union gunboat. After allowing the eleven prisoners to watch the destruction of their vessel, he sent them below under armed guard and put the brig back on course for Chesapeake Bay.

The tenor of the voyage had changed in character with their approach to the Yankee coast. The men suddenly came alive with a renewed sense of purpose, and as events progressed at an ever faster pace their determination grew along with their fear of capture. Of chief importance was the disposing of the prisoners and keeping a low profile, difficult to do under the circumstances but not impossible. As aboard *Florida*, the presence of Yankees taken off their ships and seething with rage about their misfortune posed a danger. In enemy waters, the risk increased markedly. If boarders from a Union cruiser came alongside, the men of *Clarence* knew they would find themselves in the same unpleasant position their unwilling passengers currently endured.

The following morning, the raider overhauled a neutral vessel, the brig *Argus*, bound from Havana to Antwerp. After a protracted conversation with Read, the Dutch master of the brig agreed to take Captain Butler and three of his men aboard in return for three coils of spun yarn, one barrel of beef, one barrel of bread, and two kegs of nails. The cost was high, given the relative shortage of supplies, but Read accepted the Dutchman's terms. He still had seven men from *Whistling Wind* left to dispose of. At least the number of prisoners was significantly reduced. Indeed, prisoners were a problem he resolved to deal with as best he could without curtailing his destruction of Union shipping. Killing the Yankees and throwing them overboard would have been an easy solution to the issue. However, barbarous acts defied international law. There was another reason too, which Mrs. Williams of *Jacob Bell* expressed rather well:

Although outwardly civil, it required no extraordinary power to see plainly that, could it have served their purpose and benefited their cause, it would have cost them no pang to act the pirate to the *death*, as they were acting it to the life; but to carry their feelings of hatred to such an extent, they well knew, would array the whole civilized world against them.

Thus, Read accepted the risks involved in putting the prisoners aboard neutral ships, and later aboard prizes he bonded, allowing the captains to proceed with their voyages after signing a pledge promising payment to the Confederate States of America thirty days after the war ended. Reflecting the general feeling of the rebel sailors, as *Argus* filled away on a course that would take her across the Atlantic Ocean, Drayton wrote: "They are bound for Antwerp. Hope they will not meet a vessel to take them off [before they reach Belgium]."

Later in the day, *Clarence*'s men pursued and brought to an American schooner with every intention of burning her. This vessel was loaded with a cargo of guns and clothing for the "loyal citizens of the Confederate States of America," Read wrote in his report. Both schooner and cargo belonged to a traitorous New York–based businessman named Diller. He was bound for Matamoros, a once sleepy Mexican seaport on the Rio Grande across from Brownsville, Texas. After the war started, it quickly transformed into a major trading center for the Confederacy. As a foreign port, it could not be blockaded and offered a lucrative and relatively safe inlet for shipments to Southern states. Unscrupulous merchants in the North like Diller sent supplies into Matamoros, earning handsome profits paid in gold on each venture. These men were an unsavory bunch, like those aboard Diller's schooner, *Alfred H. Partridge*. Even the sailors aboard *Clarence* considered them bad characters, for several of the worst hard cases were known to a crewman who had spent nearly a decade as a police officer in New Orleans before he joined *Florida*.

"[They] are of the desperate class. In fact, the whole of the crew, one murderer amongst them . . . The Capt., Mr. R., sent for the owner, Mr. D., and satisfied him[self] that he was all right," Drayton wrote.

Diller and Read agreed on mutually

acceptable terms, the former pledging a bond of $5,000 payable to the Confederacy when peace was declared. Diller also agreed to take the seven prisoners to Mexico. Many of Read's crew hastily wrote letters to their loved ones at home, including Drayton. It was difficult for them to cruise the high seas without much prospect of returning to the Confederacy. They wondered what had become of their families, how the war progressed, and all of them wished for peace, though on terms agreeable to them, not to Uncle Abe, as they called President Lincoln.

In addition to taking the prisoners and the mail, Diller gave Read the latest newspapers from New York. Together with those taken from *Whistling Wind*, he gleaned an inkling of the tidings from home. News from the western theater indicated that Vicksburg remained in Confederate hands. Given the importance of this stronghold, the report contributed to the celebratory mood of the men. "Got news from New York to June 1st. Vicksburg is not taken yet, nor likely to be [unintelligible] for little Vick with hospitable hands she has welcomed them [Union soldiers] to bloody graves. . . . If the Yankees are defeated, I think the war is ended," Drayton wrote.

Apart from carrying out his secondary mission to destroy American merchant ships "en route," as Maffitt specified in his orders, unknown to his men Read was gathering intelligence for the main objective, his attack on the shipping in Hampton Roads and the "cutting out" of a Union gunboat or steamship. He studied the newspapers and also interrogated the prisoners to find out as much as he could about the defenses around Fortress Monroe. His discoveries disturbed him. He began to question the wisdom of his own proposal. The Union defenses were strong indeed, stronger than he initially thought. Nevertheless, he was determined to attack.

With the wind blowing fresh from the northwest, Read set a course for the brig nearly due west direct for Cape Fear. The wind would likely back to the west and south in the next day or two and enable him to make good his northing on a fast point of sail. Every hour brought the brig closer to land, and soon the meandering eddies of the Gulf Stream surrounded the vessel, changing the color of the sea to a brilliant turquoise. Some of the men drew buckets of seawater to the deck and found the water far warmer than it had been in recent days. They did not need a thermometer to discern the difference, and even the landsmen among them knew what it meant. The word spread among them. They were in the Gulf Stream. As the sun settled below the horizon dead off the bow, the warning Diller gave Read within earshot of his crew lingered in their minds. "You're getting too far north, Lieutenant. It's going to get pretty messy for you if you don't turn back."

Retreat was out of the question. Nothing would convince Read to do that, nothing short of capture or death.

President Lincoln appointed Gideon Welles to his cabinet as secretary of the navy. At the start of the American Civil War, fewer than 100 ships were in active service. By 1865, the fleet numbered more than 600 vessels charged with enforcing the blockade, fighting Confederate forces on inland waterways, and hunting commerce destroyers on the high seas. Welles's long white beard and his wig of gray hair earned him the nickname of Father Neptune. President Lincoln, who considered Welles a close friend, called him Uncle Gideon.

This photograph was taken of Charles W. Read after he graduated from the Naval Academy in Annapolis in June 1860. He resigned his commission in the spring of 1861 to join the Confederate Navy and became one of the most daring officers of the service.

Almost immediately upon joining the Confederate Navy as a second lieutenant, Charles W. Read served with valor aboard CSS *McRae* at the Battle of New Orleans in April 1862. After the captain was mortally wounded, Read took command and fought the attacking Union fleet until the ship was disabled. He engaged the same Union fleet on July 15, 1862, aboard the ironclad CSS *Arkansas,* shown here in action on the Mississippi River above the Confederate stronghold of Vicksburg.

This painting shows CSS *Florida* running the Union blockade at Mobile Bay on September 4, 1862. Safe in the strongly defended Confederate port, *Florida*'s commander, John Newland Maffitt, readied the ship for use as a commerce destroyer. He had heard of Lieutenant Read's courage and coolness under fire on the Mississippi River, and had him assigned for duty aboard *Florida*. Maffitt led the vessel back through the Union blockade on January 6, 1863, and began sinking Yankee merchant ships.

Courtesy of The Mariners' Museum,
Newport News, Virginia

The Confederate Navy inflicted the most harm on the Union through its use of commerce destroyers. These swift, well-armed ships burned, bonded, or captured more than 200 Yankee merchant vessels. John Newland Maffitt, seen here in a photograph, was one of the most successful raiders during the Civil War. He became a mentor for Lieutenant Read, who greatly admired him as *Florida*'s commander.

The waters off Brazil represented a crossroads for shipping and attracted Confederate commerce destroyers. This illustration shows *Florida* with a prize captured on May 6, 1863, the brig *Clarence* (left). Maffitt gave Lieutenant Read the brig for use as a raider, outfitting the ship with one small cannon and a handful of men. Read then embarked on one of the most daring raids of the Civil War.

While the Navy was succeeding in its overall objectives, the land war went badly for the Union in 1862. Confederate forces continued to win major battles. Hoping to convince the eleven Confederate states to return to the Union, President Lincoln on September 22, 1862, issued the Emancipation Proclamation in preliminary form. It would free all slaves in Confederate states in active rebellion on January 1, 1863, if those states failed to rejoin the Union. They refused. This painting shows the first reading of the Proclamation in the presence of Lincoln's cabinet. Gideon Welles is seated next to Lincoln.

199

Cries of outrage about the Confederate raiders filled the pages of newspapers up and down the coast. State and local government officials, merchants, shipowners, and insurance underwriters petitioned Gideon Welles for help to catch them. Welles dispatched additional ships. Nevertheless, Welles was harshly criticized in the press. It was not the first time, nor the last. This cartoon of Welles, the "Old Man of the Sea," riding atop "Sinbad" Lincoln's shoulders, was published in *Frank Leslie's Illustrated Newspaper* in May 1862, after the battle between the *Monitor* and *Merrimac* (CSS *Virginia*) on March 9.

200

On June 12, 1863, while cruising about forty-five miles off Chesapeake Bay, Lieutenant Read captured the bark *Tacony*. He transferred his men from *Clarence* to her, correctly believing she was a faster ship. While in the process of moving his command aboard *Tacony*, two other Yankee traders sailed near. Read captured them as well.

Courtesy of The Maine Historical Society

Read learned of the dragnet of more than twenty Union warships out looking for him from newspapers taken off captured ships. Instead of turning back for the safety of the Confederacy, he kept sailing north. On June 20, he was off Nantucket, where he decimated the fishing fleet. Foggy weather helped him elude the Union vessels searching for him. This illustration shows *Tacony* sailing among the fishing schooners.

By June 24, 1863, Lieutenant Read and his men had sailed from Brazil all the way to the waters off Nova Scotia, capturing, burning or bonding twenty-one Union vessels. Read knew Union cruisers were in hot pursuit and that the captains had a good description of *Tacony*. He switched vessels yet again, this time to a fishing schooner called *Archer*. This illustration shows *Archer* sailing away, with *Tacony* in flames behind her. Read headed for Portland, Maine, where he captured the revenue cutter *Caleb Cushing* and escaped to sea with her.

Courtesy of The Maine Historical Society

After an exchange of cannon fire with pursuing Union steamers, Lieutenant Read realized he faced imminent capture. Instead of surrendering *Caleb Cushing*, he blew her up, taking to the small boats just minutes before the massive explosion. A local artist made this engraving showing the blast shortly after the dramatic event. Eventually, the image was sold as a souvenir.

Chapter Eleven

ENEMIES DRAW NEAR

Welles Residence, Washington, D.C., June 10, 1863

A swirl of blue-gray smoke ascended from the bowl of Gideon Welles's favorite clay pipe. The rising tendril, backlit by the dim light of the lamp on the desk, hung motionless for a moment before it dissipated. The heavy, almost sweet, odor of Virginia tobacco filled the study and the familiar aroma helped Welles relax. He wiped sweat from his brow and glanced toward the open window. The thick curtains needed in winter to reduce drafts were pulled all the way back, but no breeze entered the room. He resigned himself to the arrival of the stifling summer heat, an oppression he was forced to endure as long as his duty kept him and Mary in Washington. At times like these, he missed Hartford and the southerly winds blowing inland from Long Island Sound that cooled the house after sunset.

Late at night, engaged in his nocturnal routine of writing in his diary, Welles allowed himself another personal comfort. After the servants all retired, he removed his wig. He looked rather odd without it, somehow out of balance, the roundness of his nearly bald head draped at the curve of his jaw with a long white beard below his clean-shaven upper lip. It was as if the wig and beard provided a mask to hide behind, one that contributed to the inscrutable facet of his outward appearance as perceived by others. He knew people called him Father Neptune and that Abraham Lincoln affectionately referred to him as Uncle Gideon. Neither nickname bothered him much, nor did it matter to him that friends and colleagues found his waves of slightly curled fake hair amusing. There were many individuals in Washington with stranger ways and quirks more pronounced than his. He tolerated slight leeway in the conduct of his life. A little vanity, though a sin, was a failing of character he accepted in his personal makeup.

Welles drew on his pipe, the ember brightening in the bowl. He leaned back and savored the smoke before he exhaled.

The year had been eventful and much had been accomplished. Vicksburg was on the verge of falling, at last. The blockade was now quite effective; its prolonged chokehold on the South was having the desired effect. The rebel troops were short of supplies, but still managed to procure powder and weapons to continue their struggle. The Union losses suffered at Fredericksburg and, more recently, Chancellorsville, while staggering, also slowly sapped the strength from General Robert E. Lee's proud Army of Northern Virginia. As Lincoln was fond of saying, the "arithmetic" favored the North. It appeared in theory that the South, outnumbered and outgunned, must lose the war. Just when that might occur, however, was anybody's guess, and theories did not necessarily translate into reality.

Welles yawned and looked down at the pages of his diary. The entry for June 10 was shorter than most; it nevertheless revealed the two main concerns he had brought home that day from the Navy Department. The first involved rumors of a major cavalry engagement near Culpeper, Virginia, at a place called Brandy Station. A massive number of rebel horsemen under command of General J. E. B. Stuart were on the move and had been surprised in the field. Intelligence from observers, aloft in Army reconnaissance balloons at the front along the shores of the Rappahannock River near Fredericksburg, indicated on June 4 that some of the rebel army had withdrawn. No one knew exactly where they were or what they were up to, though it was thought the force was headed west.

The rumors were beginning to focus on yet another invasion of the North, but Welles did not place much stock in them. The more logical reason for the disappearance of the troops would be a long and desperate attempt to reinforce Vicksburg. Indeed, the Confederate government did consider the option before deciding to send Lee north, at Lee's most ardent insistence. Still, it was disconcerting to consider that Lee might advance again into the border states and proceed toward the heart of the Union, cutting off Washington in the process. The ghosts of Lee's last foray in September loomed large enough for Lincoln and Secretary of War Edwin M. Stanton to hasten from Washington to visit General "Fighting Joe" Hooker at army headquarters in Falmouth, or so Welles thought on the evening of June 10. (Lincoln had actually gone to Fort Lyon, near Alexandria.)

Of more immediate concern to Welles on this night was his mounting frustration regarding the Confederate commerce destroyers, and the reasons efforts to apprehend them continued to fail. The ongoing depredations were only one cause of his consternation. More acute were his feelings of disgust with Rear Admiral Charles Wilkes, commander of the West India Squadron. Pressure from England, Spain, Mexico, and Denmark coming through diplomatic channels regarding Wilkes's abuse of the laws of neutrality had reached the point where action was required. As usual, Britain threatened war. It was becoming tiring to Welles, their constant saber rattling and pomp. This latest threat arose because of Wilkes's transgressions in the West Indies, largely his pursuit of suspected blockade runners sailing under the protection of the British ensign. Some of these infractions were real, and others mere fabrications of the British to make Wilkes's position untenable and his ability to pursue the Confederate commerce destroyers as difficult as possible.

It is best under the circumstances that Wilkes should be withdrawn from the

West Indies, where he was sent by [Secretary of State William H.] Seward's special request, unless, as he says, we are ready for a war with England. I sometimes think that is not the worst alternative, she behaves so badly.

Throughout the rebellion, the fear of war with England was real and, at times, palpable. Seward tended to exaggerate the threat and Welles tended to meet it with a bellicosity to match the British tit for tat. As secretary of state, Seward's influence concerning foreign affairs generally held sway and Lincoln, with the exception of the issue pertaining to letters of marque, sanctioned a policy of appeasement. It seemed that Wilkes had played into Britain's hands, which Welles found disturbing, though predictable.

What really angered Welles, beyond the political games centered around Wilkes and his questionable interactions with foreign powers, was the admiral's disregard of orders. On many occasions, Welles noted in his diary Wilkes's tendency to obey orders only when they cohered to his point of view. He also noted with irritation Wilkes's constant carping for more resources that simply were not available, as Du Pont had done with regard to the botched affair at Charleston. A study of Welles's writings presents a slow and steady escalation of his antipathy. Although he was a politician at heart, Welles believed in the rule of authority with militaristic fervor, and to have a subordinate flout it proved entirely unacceptable, particularly when it led to the escape of the most notorious Confederate raider afloat, Raphael Semmes and his much feared cruiser, *Alabama*. The lapse in discipline led to further bad press and criticism in the halls of Congress that reflected on Welles personally, fueling his anger. It was an affront to the efficiency of his department. On May 29, Welles wrote:

We have accounts of farther and extensive depredations by the Alabama. These depredations were near the Line, where the Department, in anticipation of her appearance, had ordered the Vanderbilt. She was specially ordered to Fernando de Noronha, whither the Alabama was expected to go, — where she did go, and where she would have been captured, had instructions been obeyed, and not interfered with. But Admiral Wilkes, having fallen in with that vessel and finding her a commodious ship with extensive and comfortable accommodations, deliberately annexed her to his squadron and detained her in the West Indies as his flagship, hunting prizes, too long for the service on which she was specially sent. I, of course, shall be abused for the escape of the Alabama and her destruction of property by those who know nothing of the misconduct of Wilkes. The propriety of recalling that officer is more apparent than ever. He has accomplished nothing, but has sadly interrupted and defeated the plans of the Department.

On June 1, Welles met with Commodore James L. Lardner, Wilkes's replacement, prior to his departure for the West Indies to take over the squadron. They talked at length about Lardner's mission, and how he might avoid a repetition of Wilkes's snags with foreign powers over the rights of neutrals. Excluding *Vanderbilt*, Lardner's command consisted of eleven vessels, hardly a sufficient number to patrol the Caribbean Sea, yet he would have to try. In his instructions, Welles warned of the latest intelligence received regarding the rebels' new practice of converting prizes into raiders, which he heard about through

Captain Glisson's dispatches from Pernambuco and other sources. "In all probability they will be converted into cruisers to depredate on our commerce, possibly to make a descent upon the coast at some unprotected point. Should this latter scheme be attempted, the marauders will be likely to rendezvous, preparatory to offensive operations, somewhere in the West Indies."

While Welles lacked seamanship and combat skills, he appeared to have been a quick study, demonstrating at least a rudimentary knowledge of the rebel captains. Based on his assessment of their possible actions, he took most but not all of the necessary steps to stop them. Had Wilkes not claimed *Vanderbilt* as his flagship, and instead sent her to Fernando de Noronha as Welles instructed, *Alabama* and *Florida* might have been caught. It was not an overestimation on Welles's part to have thought so. Each of the raiders called there at the time *Vanderbilt* should have been on station waiting for them, and her speed and guns were superior to those of both rebel cruisers. It was indeed vexing to Welles to have lost the opportunity to grab them, and costly to the Union economy as well.

Welles's instructions to Lardner demonstrated another insight: that the rebel captains might consider attacking merchantmen in the coastal waters of the United States, just as Massachusetts's Governor Andrew predicted and warned of in late April. It was an accurate sentiment, based on logical conclusions. Earlier in the war, in its first days, Confederate privateers had ranged north, though they did little harm and were promptly sunk. It was no flash of genius to think Jefferson Davis and his naval secretary, Stephen R. Mallory, would find an assault on the coast useful propaganda. There was a growing peace movement afoot in the Union, spurred by the economic interests of the rich, and given further impetus by the institution of the draft. The financial losses from a coastal rampage were also potentially enormous. Together, these might help ignite a concerted thrust to petition for a cessation of hostilities that would result in the destruction of the Union. Lee's current march north toward Gettysburg, of which Welles and the rest of Washington would soon learn, was undertaken for similar reasons. Had Lee succeeded in that terrible battle less than a month away, the outcome of the war might well have been different.

Welles now believed a threat to the coast

was more realistic, in view of the growing number of cruisers the Confederates had acquired through capture and purchases in England. But try as he would, he remained one step behind them. No rendezvous was planned for the West Indies. The rendezvous Maffitt and Read hoped to make off Nantucket appeared unthinkable to Welles. He also did not redeploy any forces to cover the coast, as he should have done were he to guard against all contingencies — those unexpected surprises the Confederates frequently dished up for Welles's counterparts in the War Department.

The hour grew late, as Welles sat behind his desk in those quiet, most favored hours of the day on June 10. The press of his duties kept his keen mind working long after his strength flagged and a need for sleep caused his eyes to flutter and shut. He looked over the last lines he had written: "The accounts of piratical depredations disturb me. . . . The Rebel cruisers are now beginning to arm their prizes and find adventurers to man them. Our *neutral* friends will be likely to find the police of the seas in a bad way."

Indeed. The police of the seas. Lawlessness reigned as the raiders multiplied. The police of the seas, he thought, closing his diary. The police of the seas . . .

The warm summer breeze blowing from the south sped the bark *Almona* on her way to New York. Outbound from Shanghai loaded with a cargo of tea, her passage had been swift. Her captain cracked on all sail as the ship closed with the flat, sandy shoreline of New Jersey. He had reason to hurry beyond the usual competition among tea packet companies to bring their cargoes home at the fastest possible speed. He had spoken to the German brig *Argus*, bound for Antwerp, and taken aboard a number of crewmen, including the captain, of a vessel recently destroyed off the Carolina coast. The news of a Confederate raider so far north shocked him. However, as he listened to the story of Captain Butler, late of the bark *Whistling Wind*, he entertained no doubts about the validity of his tale and its implications to merchants from Philadelphia to Portland, Maine. According to Butler, the captain of the commerce destroyer was steering a northerly course and probably had been since June 6, the day the rebels torched his ship.

The tea packet made her way past Sandy Hook into the lower bay of New York on the morning of June 11. Under the guidance of a pilot, she headed north up the Main Ship Channel to her berth on the East River. She joined her graceful sisters crowded against the piers. Forests of masts rose skyward, and bowsprits and jibbooms projected over the busy streets along the waterfront with its squat, three-story brick shops and warehouses. *Almona* carried more than just a valuable cargo. She brought with her the first news to reach the Union about a rebel pirate heading north. It induced among mariners the same response that might be expected of swimmers at the beach on hearing that a shark had suddenly surfaced in their midst.

Chapter Twelve

DEADLY STRIKE

At Sea, 40 Miles Due East of Chesapeake Bay, 5:30 a.m., June 12, 1863

The early morning sun hung low over the horizon off *Clarence*'s stern, casting the smooth mounds of the waves washing under the transom in the shiny, mercurylike hue common at sea before the full brightness of the day commenced in earnest and turned to glare. Off the bow, in the long shadows of the sails, the ocean retained its darkness. The black expanse broke occasionally from the hiss and surge of white foam on either side of the ship as she rose and fell to the procession of swells rolling toward the broad mouth of Chesapeake Bay. She had passed through the Gulf Stream and drew closer to shore every hour. The passage westward toward land represented a circumstance many of the men considered with trepidation, still unaware of why they cruised into danger, their captain's secret still kept.

"There seems to be a universal feeling of the close proximity of the land and a general fear of capture," Drayton wrote the previous evening. Lending credence to the source of anxiety among the crew, the sudden appearance of a large, lead-colored steamship all believed was a Yankee cruiser inspired most of them to rush below to gather their few belongings in case Read ordered the ship fired to keep her from the enemy. The strange, imposing vessel changed course and steamed off the brig's bow. She then proceeded on her way, her master satisfied that the Union merchantman posed no threat and was not worthy of boarding for an examination of her papers. Her lines bore the distinctive design features found in New England. She looked harmless from a distance, her Quaker guns run in and hidden from view, the little howitzer under its canvas tarp, and the Stars and Stripes flying aloft.

Clarence cruised within a half-day's sail of Fortress Monroe, a somber presence perched on the north side of Hampton Roads on Old Point Comfort, a fleet of supply vessels safe under the protection of the gun batteries. The Elizabeth River and the city of Norfolk, with more ships anchored close in deep water, lay to the south, and, beyond Newport News Point, the James River cut inland into Virginia. Farther north, the mouths of the York, Rappahannock, and Potomac opened to the long funnel of the bay reaching more than two hundred miles to Baltimore, the place Read had wished to attack when he first proposed the mission to Maffitt. Hot as he was to strike deep in Union territorial waters, Read had not at first understood why Maffitt countermanded his request to dash so far into the confines of the shoal-strewn Chesapeake. Now that he possessed his own command, and the burden of responsibility for the lives of his men, the merits of caution began to impress him.

Read had obtained newspapers from the neutral ships he had hailed since June 6. He also had those from *Whistling Wind*, and the brig *Mary Alvina*, captured and burned on June 9. These combined reports provided evidence concerning the poor odds of success for any raid into Hampton Roads. The prisoners of *Mary Alvina*, all huddled below under armed guard, said very little in answer to his interrogations, just as those of *Whistling Wind* remained mostly silent. Some of the men were politely persuaded to talk, and gave Read a clear idea of what to expect should he sail past Cape Henry and make for Fortress Monroe.

From the prisoners and papers of the transports [*Whistling Wind*] and *Mary Alvina* I derived such information as convinced me that it was impossible to carry out the instructions of Commander Maffitt. No vessels were allowed to go into Hampton Roads unless they had supplies for the U.S. Government, and then they were closely watched. The vessels lying at the wharf above Fortress Monroe were guarded by a gunboat, and there were sentries on the wharf. Just outside the fort there were two boarding steamers.

The important question in Read's mind, upon receipt of this intelligence, was whether he should trust it. Disinformation and deception were common in war. He played that game himself. It was possible that the defenses were not as strong as the prisoners made them out to be, but then again, they might have told him the truth.

He had learned much in the five weeks he commanded *Clarence*. While he did not wish to spend his men on a useless errand, he nevertheless wanted to carry on with his mission. Based on what he learned, it seemed obvious he could not sail into Hampton Roads with *Clarence*. "I then determined to cruise along the coast and try to intercept a transport for Fortress Monroe and with her to endeavor to carry out the orders of Commander Maffitt, and in the meantime to do all possible injury to the enemy's commerce."

If *Clarence* were to meet with a transport bound for Hampton Roads, she would have to cruise in the approaches to the Yankee stronghold. Thus, Read made his northing well offshore and proceeded west along latitude 37 degrees north, headed straight toward the bay. The mission to destroy commerce was secondary, but one he was determined to execute with vigor, should the opportunity favor him. They had been lucky so far, very lucky. He overheard the men saying *Florida*'s uncanny good fortune traveled with them; this seemed to help assuage their fear of capture, which Read knew permeated the ship, and for good reason.

As Read stood on his little bridge, the

sun to his back, he continued to observe the sleek, black bark sailing northward off his port beam. She was approximately 375 tons displacement, almost twice the size of *Clarence*, with a lofty rig, a yellow figure-head at the prow, and intricate carvings painted white along her stern. She sailed much faster than *Clarence* and on her present course might pass the brig before the two vessels crossed paths. If that occurred, there was no hope of catching her. Read turned to First Officer Brown. "Call all hands to quarters," he said, "but keep the guns under cover."

"Aye, sir," Brown said.

Read also ordered the colors half-masted and any crewmen wearing the uniform of the Confederate Navy to disguise it in favor of the garb of the usual Yankee sailor. The ruse had worked well with *Whistling Wind*. It might do so again.

The men tumbled to in well-practiced fashion. The long hours of drills beneath the intense tropical sun that once seemed amusing and ridiculous had transformed them into a combat-ready team. That all the guns, save one, were wood did not matter. The thrill and rush of battle took hold every time the brig hove close to a potential prize, and it was no different on this morning, the air still cool from the receding cloak of darkness, yet tinged with the promise of the coming heat of the day. The crew stood in silence and watched as the bark approached. Closer. Closer she sailed, until the faces of the men on her deck were easily discerned. The bark changed course and the two ships sailed side by side. At exactly 6:00 a.m., Read raised his speaking trumpet.

"Ahoy, Captain!" Read shouted, his soft voice barely able to carry across the wide slot of water separating the ships. "We are the brig *Clarence*, bound for Baltimore."

"Bark *Tacony*, from Port Royal to Philadelphia, Captain," replied William G. Mundy, master of *Tacony*. "What is the nature of your distress?"

"Have you water to spare? Our supply is exhausted," Read said.

Mundy later reported in detail what happened next.

Of course I hauled to on this appeal to humanity, and their boat, with an officer and six men immediately came aboard. They told me they were fifty-five days from Rio de Janeiro, were bound to Baltimore, and were entirely out of water, and would assist me in passing it to the boat. While taking the after hatch off, I was confronted by the officer of the boat, who presented a pistol at my head, and stated that my vessel was his prize, a prize to the Confederate States. . . .

As with the two previous captures, the ships lay to while the Yankee crew gathered their belongings and were transferred to *Clarence*. A thorough search of the bark revealed she was homeward bound, in ballast, after delivering a cargo of coal to the Union fleet stationed at Port Royal, South Carolina. In his private cabin, Read examined the ship's log and a plan formed in his mind, as he noted with pleasure the fast daily runs Mundy had recorded. *Tacony* was indeed a superior vessel. A cry from aloft brought him swiftly back topsides.

"Sail ho!" the lookout shouted.

Read snapped his glass to his eye and made the vessel out as a schooner several miles distant on a northerly heading.

"We will get underway, Mr. Brown," he said. "Get those prisoners below."

Leaving a prize crew aboard *Tacony*, the remainder of the crew cleared for action, running the Quaker guns out and manning the howitzer. The prisoners of *Tacony* joined those of *Mary Alvina* below decks under a doubled armed guard. From their vantage point in the dark, odiferous hold, they saw nothing of what transpired on deck. However, they all knew their captors pursued yet another vessel and hoped they would fail to catch her. All settled down in a tense state of quiet. Time passed. The suspense of the moment caused many of them to sweat, their hearts to pound. The boom of a cannon startled the prisoners. The stamp of feet running on deck, the bang and clatter of blocks, and the thunder of canvas luffing to the wind as the brig's topsails went aback told them all was not well for their countrymen. In a short time, they welcomed additional prisoners into their ranks, and most wondered what the raider's small, uncommunicative captain had in store for them.

Up on deck, Read surveyed his second prize of what was becoming a very pleasant day, the schooner *M. A. Shindler*, as his men sailed her in company back to *Tacony*, which remained hove to. The three ships lay together, rolling and pitching a short distance apart on the swells, their sails backed and their decks cleared of all but loyal citizens of the Confederate States of America. For a long moment, the rebel sailors all peered at each other from their respective posts aboard the three ships formerly of the United States. They looked to Read for instructions.

"The bark *Tacony* being a better sailer than the *Clarence*, I determined to burn the latter vessel and take the bark," Read wrote in his official report of the action.

Read relayed his orders to Brown and the petty officers, and the men set to work. Some of them rigged block and tackle to lower away the crates of ammunition for the small arms, shot, cartridge bags, powder, and the howitzer. Others in shifts shuttled to *Clarence*, grabbed their duffel, and brought it to *Tacony*. The gun crew trundled the howitzer to the weather deck and lashed it in preparation for hoisting into a longboat. They cursed and groaned as they manhandled the gun, which weighed over seven hundred pounds, and hauled taut the lines to raise it over the bulwarks. Slowly and carefully, they slacked the lines and the cannon inched downward.

"Easy, boys," the officer in charge said. "Easy does it."

Lowering the cannon proved difficult. The men timed the rise and fall of the boat with those on deck handling the lines. One moment the boat rose high and the gun was inside it, and the next the boat dropped into the trough and the gun teetered and swung in midair, crashing against the side of the brig. At last, they timed it right, and let go the falls when the gun found its place in the bottom of the boat. They unshipped the oars and pulled away to *Tacony*.

"Sail ho! . . . Captain, a schooner bears down on us!" the lookout yelled.

Read turned his attention from the boat sunk low under the weight of the howitzer to the sail that had come up surprisingly fast, unnoticed until she drew quite close. Read made her out as another Yankee, an old-looking schooner sailing before the wind, her master evidently curious about why three ships lay hove to.

While the howitzer, etc., was being transferred from the *Clarence* to the *Tacony*, a schooner was discovered coming down before the wind. Passing near the *Clarence*, a wooden gun was pointed at her, and she was commanded to heave to, which she did immediately. She was found to be the schooner *Kate Stewart*, from Key West to Philadelphia, in ballast.

The master of *Kate Stewart* was terrified

at the sight of the Quaker guns. Believing they were real, he cried out: "For God's sake, don't fire! I surrender!"

Now four ships lay hove to, making a very suspicious sight for any Union cruisers that might have chanced by. All the prisoners were herded together on *Clarence*'s weather deck, save those of *Kate Stewart*, who remained on their vessel under guard. A head count indicated more than fifty of them. Outnumbering the rebels two to one, they posed a threat to the safety of Read's men. If they chose to resist, it was possible for them to overpower the crew and retake the ship. Just like Maffitt and Semmes, Read preferred to dispose of prisoners as quickly as possible. To complicate matters further, some of the passengers aboard *Kate Stewart* were female. At about noon, two more vessels, hull down below the horizon, hove into view.

As we were now rather short of provisions and had over fifty prisoners, I determined to bond the schooner *Kate Stewart* and make a cartel of her. I bonded her for the sum of $7,000, payable to the President of the Confederate States thirty days after the ratification of a treaty of peace between the Confederate States and the United States. The brig *Clarence* and the schooner *Shindler* were then set on fire. We now stood in chase of a brig. . . .

The flames quickly spread across the decks and ignited the tar on the standing rigging, traveling along the yards to set the sails ablaze. Gray smoke blew off to leeward thick enough to reduce visibility. The crackle, hiss, and sputter of the fire carried across the water and combined together into a dull roar. As pieces of rigging, spars, and sails dropped into the sea, puffs of steam erupted from the backs of the swells. The masts toppled one by one, lying in the water, battering the hulls before snapping free and floating away.

Read's men hesitated, observing the results of their morning's work. But soon they manned their sail stations, hauled the braces round, as the helmsman spun the wheel. The wind filled the topsails and the bark came nimbly to her new heading. Men climbed aloft to set additional canvas. *Tacony* heeled to the wind, speeding through the swells with a steady rush of spray at her cutwater.

The schooner *Kate Stewart* filled away as well, the wind favoring a northward heading to Delaware Bay. People crowded her decks and discovered they had nowhere else to go to find shelter from the elements. There was not enough room for them all below, and the master hoped no foul weather came in before he brought his vessel safely to port in New Castle, Delaware. An angry sea washing over the bulwarks and across the decks would doubtless claim any number of the unfortunate passengers. This was a distinct possibility. In a strong northeasterly with a flood tide, the waters of Delaware Bay became vicious. He had no choice about exposing the innocents to danger. The rebels had seen to that.

The morning's events altered Read's intended variation on the original mission, making the decision for him concerning how to proceed next. He understood that tarrying in these waters in the hope of seizing a transport bound for Fortress Monroe no longer made sense. Union warships would soon be sent to hunt him down; it was only a matter of when. By his best estimates, he could make the planned-for rendezvous with *Florida* off Nantucket, if she indeed was on her way. He kept this option in mind, but concentrated on what had become his primary mission. Having abandoned all hope of raiding the shipping in Hampton Roads, he intended to destroy every Yankee vessel that sailed within range of his howitzer. With the swift bark *Tacony*, he was sanguine about the prospects for mass destruction. He squinted through the lens of his glass at the brig off the bow, pleased at how she appeared to loom closer with each passing minute.

After the men stowed their belongings, Read called all hands aft. They gathered together, braced to the motion of the ship as she surged through the waves, the fresh wind a low moan in the rigging, the patter of spray tapping the forecastle deck on its windward side. Astern, a cloud of gray and black smoke rose from the sea. In his hand, he held a slender envelope. With ceremony, he broke the seal in front of the men, telling them to listen well to the words of Captain Maffitt, and explaining for the first time what had brought them to these waters and what he intended to do next. The men looked from one to the other, astonished and strangely calm. Drayton wrote:

After we got aboard the bark and set the vessels afire, he [Read] mustered all hands and read to us his instructions from Capt. Maffitt. The plan as laid down was certainly a bold one but I must say a reckless one and can not approve of it. It was impossible for any one to conceive it and had we been successful, the Yanks would have opened their eyes and thought hell was certainly broke loose, time will tell what will be our fate as for me I have a heart for every fate, a fear for those [who] love me, a smile for those [who] hate.

Tacony sailed fast on a north-northeasterly course through the rest of the afternoon, dogging the brig as a wolf shadows a deer. It was no easy task for a sailing ship to gain ground on another of similar speed, if the chase enjoyed a significant head start, as this brig did. Yet Read kept after her, as tenacious as ever, perhaps driven beyond his earlier zeal out of frustration at being turned away from Hampton Roads by the preparedness of the Union and the bad luck in not catching a ship with the appropriate papers to allow him to skirt the defensive shield. As the hours passed, the lookouts spotted a Union cruiser making way at flank speed to the south. The presence of the gunboat, so near while they were on the chase, alarmed some of the men, but they need not have worried too much. Like *Clarence* before her, *Tacony* appeared harmless, just another Yankee trader. The advantage was great, for neither the commander of the gunboat nor the merchant captain of the brig off the bow suspected her.

Soon, the advantage would no longer hold in *Tacony*'s favor, and all her company knew it. When *Kate Stewart* made port and the prisoners raised the alarm, Union warships would have a fine description of the bark. However, that eventuality lay over the horizon at least a day or so away. Although Read did not know it, his transfer to *Tacony* nullified the news published that same day in New York from the prisoners of *Whistling Wind*, alerting the U.S. Navy and the U.S. Merchant Marine of a dark-hulled brig named *Clarence* steering north to continue her attacks. Any ships seeking the brig would never find her, and the accounts of *Clarence* created confusion among certain Union captains, not sure if it was a brig or a bark they were hunting.

Read set the regular watches, giving the men time to rest as the bark kept hard on the heels of the chase. The sun lowered on the western horizon and the purple beauty of twilight on a warm summer's night tinged the sky to the east over the Atlantic.

Tacony sailed on and the distance between her and the brig diminished, until at 7:00 p.m., she had drawn within an eighth of a mile. They brought the brig *Arabella* to with a blank charge fired from the howitzer to conserve the dwindling supply of shot. Upon boarding the brig, preparations to burn her were begun. Her master possessed certificates proving the cargo belonged to neutral owners, so Read bonded her instead and sent her on her way. He put *Tacony* on a course due east, intending to place his ship where no one would expect to find her, far offshore outside of the Gulf Stream.

Early on the morning of June 13, a bank of clouds swept in to obscure the stars. The ocean and sky merged into an indistinguishable universe of darkness. *Tacony* sailed on, showing no lights. Showers came in, faint at first, then with more strength, and provided cover for the bark as dawn broke and she retraced the course of her doomed sister, *Clarence*, and left the Chesapeake far astern in her arrow-straight wake.

Chapter Thirteen

LIGHTNING RESPONSE

Washington, D.C., Lafayette Square, 5:00 p.m., June 13, 1863

The boisterous, brassy music of the Marine Band, one of the most popular musical groups in Washington, cheered the crowd gathered on the grounds of Lafayette Square to mark the much anticipated first performance of the summer. Ladies fanned themselves under the shade of their parasols, but found scant escape from the penetrating heat of the late afternoon, draped as they were in impossibly wide hoop skirts. Their bonnets presented an equally imposing display of flowers, velvet, and feathers, visually balancing their expansive lower proportions. Military officers with brass-buttoned and gold braided blue uniforms peppered the ranks of spectators. The civilian men wore dark suits with starched white shirts and cravats tied loosely around their necks in a reflection of the staid fashion characteristic of the utilitarian Yankee.

The people of the city craved whatever joy they might find, and the performance of the Marine Band provided a diversion from the ongoing troubles. It was particularly welcome because the previous year, these musical presentations had been canceled after the death of Willie Lincoln in February 1862. When the boy died it hurtled the president's wife, Mary, into a deep depression, and she forbade the band to play in the public park on the south side of the executive mansion. More than a year after her son's death she still could not abide the sound of music within earshot of her rooms. For a time, it looked as though the citizens of Washington might be denied the pleasure of the Marine Band performances for a second summer.

Of all the people in the close circle of Lincoln's friends, Gideon and Mary Welles best understood the pervading grief that settled over the executive mansion, an almost tangible presence in their private quarters. In those sad days in February 1862, at the Lincolns' request, Mary Welles lived with them and helped nurse Tad, who was also sick with the typhoid fever that had killed his eleven-year-old brother. Welles visited often and offered quiet reassurance to Lincoln. Mary Lincoln was frequently sedated to stave off the bouts of hysteria she experienced as a result of the stress of the grave illness of her sons, her loneliness in Washington, and her feeling of being out of place in the world in which her husband moved with shrewd ability. The war itself, apart from its immediate impact on her life, imparted its own tension, for more than a few of her relatives fought on the Confederate side. When the Welleses' son died that November the Lincolns reciprocated in giving solace to the distraught couple, thereby strengthening the growing bond between the two families.

While Welles did not enjoy as much influence over matters of policy as some of the more aggressive members of the cabinet, his friendship with Lincoln allowed him the leeway to speak frankly about a wide variety of subjects, including those that were personal in nature. The matter of the Marine Band appeared to be a rather petty issue, given the increasingly foreboding news concerning the Army of Northern Virginia's possible march north and the implications for the Union in the event Lee won yet another decisive battle. Nevertheless, Welles felt he needed to address it with the president. On Monday, June 8, Welles broached the subject:

> Spoke to the President regarding weekly performances of the Marine Band. It has been customary for them to play in the public grounds south of the Mansion once a week in summer, for many years. Last year it was intermitted, because Mrs. Lincoln objected in consequence of the death of her son. There was grumbling and discontent, and there will be more this year if the public are denied the privilege for private reasons. The public will not sympathize in sorrows which are obtrusive and assigned as a reason for depriving them of enjoyments to which they have been accustomed, and it is a mistake to persist in it. When I introduced the subject to-day, the President said Mrs. L. would not consent, certainly not until after the 4th of July. I stated the case pretty frankly, although the subject is delicate, and suggested that the band could play in Lafayette Square. . . . The President told me to do what I thought best.

With Lincoln's consent, then, Welles

arranged for the band to play in Lafayette Square and went himself, along with his wife, Assistant Secretary of the Navy Gustavas Fox, and several close friends to hear the music and to indulge in a respite from the press of business at the Navy Department. He clapped and cheered after each tune with the rest of the people in the square, and indeed the Saturday afternoon performance inspired many to forget the war for a little while. It was an especially happy day for Fox, who was celebrating his forty-second birthday.

Shortly after 5:00 p.m., Welles recognized one of his messengers pushing through the crowd. The man looked grim as he shouldered his way toward Welles, and handed him a telegram received a half hour earlier from the shipping company of E. A. Souder & Co. in Philadelphia. He scanned the few terse lines and handed the dispatch to Gustavas Fox. The celebratory mood of the afternoon was suddenly gone upon receipt of the news that a Confederate commerce destroyer had ranged north to the Chesapeake and attacked several vessels. It appeared that the anticipated arrival of these "wolves" along the shores of the United States had come at last.

"We must get every vessel in condition

to proceed to sea without delay," Welles said. "Telegraph New York and Philadelphia at once."

Fox nodded and hurried off to the Navy Department, where he spent most of the evening. Welles stayed at Lafayette Square for the rest of the performance, content to leave the matter of this rebel pirate in the capable hands of his trusted assistant.

Welles and Fox were quite different in personality and in abilities. Welles was reserved and bookish, and Fox was dynamic and prone to flamboyance. Welles was above all else a politician. Fox was a master mariner, having served in the U.S. Navy and the U.S. Merchant Marine, in the latter as captain of a mail steamer, an elite post reserved for only the best in the business. The two men complemented each other. They formed a team that proved formidable to the South and to detractors and critics in the North, and one whose efficiency tended to highlight the gross inefficiencies of their counterparts at the War Department.

Prior to the firing on Fort Sumter in April 1861, it was Fox who had spearheaded a concerted campaign to reinforce the fort. President James Buchanan had been reluctant to do so, having settled on a policy of appeasement and nonaggression, lest he find himself faced with open civil war in the last days of his watch. Others in the U.S. government, including Secretary of War John B. Floyd of Virginia, Secretary of the Interior Jacob Thompson of Mississippi, and Secretary of the Treasury Howell Cobb of Georgia, adopted a similar approach regarding their native region, even as state after state seceded from the Union and armed militia units promptly seized federal stores, arms, and fortresses. Half-hearted attempts were ultimately made to reinforce Sumter by Buchanan and Lincoln, but none succeeded.

Fox's connection with the Sumter campaign garnered the attention of powerful men in the government, not the least of whom was President Lincoln. It was at Lincoln's request that Welles appointed Fox to act as chief clerk of the Navy Department in May 1861. Welles quickly recognized Fox's energy and the soundness of his recommendations. He saw in him a man who might fill out the department, bring a mindset and expertise to it that was desperately needed. In August 1861, Welles brought his influence to bear and shepherded legislation through Congress to create a brand-new position for Fox, that of assistant secretary of the Navy, at the handsome salary of $4,000 per year. Fox earned every bit of his wages, and played a key role in planning and implementing naval operations throughout the war.

Acting under Welles's orders, Fox set in motion a massive search for *Tacony* that eventually involved close to forty vessels. Upon his arrival at the Navy Department the following day to review the dispatches sent out under his name, Welles was surprised at the breadth of the operation, and later commented on his initial reaction in his diary:

> I find that Fox, whom I authorized to telegraph to the Commandant of the Yards the other night to get off immediately vessels after the pirate Tacony, amplified the order, and that a very large number of vessels are being chartered or pressed into the service. While it was necessary to have some, there is such a thing as overdoing, but the order having gone out in my name, I could not contest it.

Welles soon changed his mind about the actions of his assistant as continued word of *Tacony*'s depredations revealed the extent to which the raider was destroying U.S. merchant ships in a trail of fire that appeared to stab northward at sea every bit as effectively as the columns of butternut-clad rebel soldiers snaked deeper and deeper into Union territory under General Robert E. Lee. Welles pursued every means to capture the raider, including arming of private vessels placed under the command of acting Navy officers and crewed by volunteers. However, that Sunday, June 14, the deployment of more than a dozen vessels to search for and destroy one rebel cruiser had struck him as excessive and a waste of naval resources.

Fox had even involved President Lincoln, asking him to authorize the deployment of the nation's revenue cutters, operating under the authority of the Treasury Department, to hunt for the rebel. Lincoln issued the order on June 14 and Secretary of the Treasury Salmon P. Chase complied. He wrote detailed orders to Captain John McGowan, commander of the U.S. Revenue Steamer Cuyahoga stationed in New York Harbor.

Like the orders issued from the Navy Department, those sent to Captain McGowan contained valuable details provided by Captain Mundy, late of the bark *Tacony*. In a lengthy dispatch sent by Mundy's employers, the owners of E. A. Souder & Co. in Philadelphia, Mundy revealed that the rebel captain, identified as Charles W. Read, a lieutenant in the Confederate Navy, disregarded all pretext of honor in favor of deception. He lured his victims by pretending his vessel was a Union merchantman in distress, and dressed his men in disguises to make them look like typical sailors. Such a practice was a violation of the spirit of international laws governing the behavior of commerce destroyers, if not a violation of the letter of the law, and it reduced Read in the view of his adversaries to nothing more than a devious criminal. Chase, therefore, included in his orders to McGowan a recommendation for appropriate action and a warning:

Obtain as exact description of the *Tacony* as possible, and proceed forthwith in search of her. As the rebels may change to another vessel or may have other vessels engaged in like depredations, you will visit every one you overhaul and satisfy yourself as to her true character, not allowing yourself to be deceived by any device, such as change of vessel, rig, paint, or flag.

Respect neutral ships and property, but capture whatever is rebel, however disguised. Conceal the warlike character of your own ship as much as may be necessary [to trick the pirates into coming close enough to bring them under your guns].

As ships put to sea from Hampton Roads, Philadelphia, New York, and Boston to search for *Tacony*, the developments inland on June 14 boded ill for the Union. In Welles's mind, they eclipsed his concerns about Read, whom he was confident would soon be caught. General Richard S. Ewell, commander of the Second Corps of the Army of Northern Virginia, in the vanguard of Lee's invasion force, began his march northward after the cavalry battle at Brandy Station, and encountered little resistance until he reached the outskirts of Winchester, Virginia on June 13. There, he found approximately five thousand Yankees under the command of Major General Robert Milroy, whom he engaged in the late afternoon of Sunday, June 14, and routed the small force with his Confederate division. The way was clear for a crossing of the Potomac, and two more divisions of Lee's army were moving in support of Ewell to bring all the might of the South to bear on the North in a grand offensive. It seemed to many in the North as they read the newspapers that a double threat had emerged at once, one by land and one by sea. The land invasion, of course, constituted the more significant threat to the Union, and it was with this in mind that Welles went to the War Department in the evening of June 14, as Milroy's men were falling prisoner to Ewell's forces, to find out the latest news from the front near Winchester.

Scary rumors abroad of army operations and a threatened movement of Lee upon Pennsylvania. . . . Found the President and General Halleck with Secretary of War [Stanton] in the room of the telegraphic operator. Stanton was uneasy, said it would be better to go into another room. The President and myself went into the Secretary's office; the other two remained. The President said quietly to me he was feeling very bad; that he found Milroy and his command were captured, or would be. . . .

Lincoln and Welles talked about the invasion that now seemed to have commenced, and both men expressed frustration at the lack of clear communication regarding the events unfolding rapidly to the west of Washington. Welles left the War Department, frowning and displeased. Once home, he wrote a long entry in his diary expressing his concerns about the way in which his peers in the War Department tended to keep matters of key importance from President Lincoln and members of the cabinet. Part of his antagonistic perspective no doubt resulted from the ongoing rivalry and incessant political intrigues that occupied much of his duty as administrator of the Navy Department, as well as his personal dislike of Stanton and Halleck. However, his observations were nevertheless a fairly accurate assessment of the state of affairs, as it became increasingly clear that Lee was on the move again and up to no good.

The President is kept in ignorance and defers to the General-in-Chief [Halleck], though not pleased that he is not fully advised of matters as they occur. There is a modest distrust of himself, of which advantage is taken. For a week, movements have been going on of which he has known none, or very few, of the details.

Welles went to sleep on that sultry

evening of June 14 with much on his mind. The war, it seemed, was about to take a decisive turn. As he settled into his bed, Mary at his side, he wondered what lay in store just over the horizon. He lay awake thinking about the war and, try as he might to banish it, a feeling of foreboding he had seldom experienced since the start of the rebellion descended over him. To the south, General Hooker's Army of the Potomac had stirred to action, and begun its fast march north to shield Washington from attack and to hunt for the nemesis that was the Army of Northern Virginia. And, far away to the east, a sleek, black bark sailed well offshore, her master hatching his latest scheme to bring the war to the heart of Yankeedom.

Chapter Fourteen

TEMPESTUOUS SEAS

At Sea, 260 Miles Southeast of Nantucket, June 16, 1863

Running before a freshening west wind and a building sea, *Tacony* sped eastward into the dull gray dawn. Thick, low clouds hung low in the sky, dark with rain that threatened to come at any moment, and cast the sea in tones of lead and black flashed white with breaking crests. The masts bowed forward under the pressure of the wind against the topgallants, topsails, and mainsail, the light sails having been clewed up and furled during the night. *Tacony* surged down the face of a large wave and buried her bow, sending cascades of green water over the weather deck to pour out the scuppers in torrents. She started to round up and the two men at the helm struggled to keep her from broaching to.

Dressed in a warm peacoat a bit too large for him, which had been acquired from the wardrobe of Captain Mundy, Read clasped the monkey rail spanning the perimeter of the poop deck to steady himself. With his back to the gale, the wind did not feel as strong as it really was. However, the high-pitched moan of the wind in the rigging, which intensified into a shriek as the gusts roared past, allowed no chance to underestimate the strength of the blow. Read glanced over at the helmsmen, coolly noting their efforts, then looked aloft again, his eyes on the topgallants. It was a risk to press on with so much sail up, yet the bark sailed with such grace and speed it seemed a pity to rein her in, like pulling up a racehorse short of a glorious run to the finish line. With the west wind, he had made up for the three days of calms, baffling breezes, most of them mere zephyrs, and the intermittent fog that obscured the sun and made it difficult for him to take his sights to determine their position.

The boisterous weather had come in the previous day and made June 15 even more eventful. For the Yankees of the brig *Umpire*, captured and burned nearly 240 miles due east of Cape Charles, it had proved rather unfortunate. She was bound for Boston from Cárdenas with a cargo of sugar and molasses, and she made for a "bully burn," as Read was fond of saying. The smoke smelled sweet as it wafted over the sea, and the cargo seemed to act as an accelerant, urged on by the stiff breeze. Drayton commented, "We sent her to keep company with several other Yankee vessels. I judge that the fishes in the ocean found their tea in that particular spot both burnt and a little too sweet."

Every mile of easting put *Tacony* farther from the Union cruisers no doubt out in force looking for her. Read shrewdly set his course to seaward under cover of the thick weather, disappearing into the vast ocean in which an entire fleet might hide without detection. As the ship flew along on the heels of the westerly, the distance from shore increased and the odds of encountering the enemy decreased. However, Read did not wish to find himself too far out to sea and have to fight his way back over several hundred miles, and with more than ten prisoners, food and water would soon run short if he was unable to get rid of his involuntary guests. Based on his dead reckoning, the rich hunting grounds off Nantucket lay less than three hundred miles off the port quarter. With no news of him since June 12, the Yankees would have no idea of where to expect him to turn up next, and it was Read's intention to give them all a terrific surprise.

In order to reduce the speed at which the storm drove them east, and to protect the ship from the high winds, Read called all hands to take in the topgallants. The sailors fought their way aloft, climbing high up the ratlines while the wind threatened to rip them from the rigging and blow them into the crests nearly one hundred feet below. They inched out on the yards and struggled with the sails, already pulled up with buntlines and clewlines to spill the air. The wind still billowed the canvas forward, though, and it took on the consistency of rock under the pressure. The best seamen Read had tried valiantly to subdue it. Eventually, they furled the canvas tight and lashed it down with the gaskets to keep it from getting loose. For some of the hands, the experience of fighting the weather instilled more fear than facing an enemy broadside. A man could fight another man and expect to equal the odds with courage and wit, but he could not expect to do so with a force as powerful as nature. The wise individuals among them understood this and took great care while executing their duty.

The ship eased under her shortened canvas, yet the helmsmen continued to work hard to keep her stern square to the gale and the rush and roar of the breaking seas sweeping toward them. Read observed the vessel, feeling at one with her, and trying to ascertain whether he should shorten her canvas still more. The mainsail, the largest one aboard, appeared ready to tear apart. The sheets and braces stretched tight enough to decrease their usual diameter. The hemp lines were strong, but they had limits. As the hours passed, with Read keeping his post on deck, the sky lightened to a pale gray and the darkness seeped away from the clouds, though the sun rising toward its zenith at local noon remained obscured behind the layer of overcast and the puffs of white scud moving fast beneath it.

"We will take in the mainsail, Mr. Brown," Read said at last.

The first officer nodded, and it was quite possible a look of relief crossed his face. This kind of work was not in the domain of an engineer, as Brown was, a man more accustomed to duty down in the hot bowels of a ship tinkering with valves, rods, and bearings to make the steam engine run without breakdowns. Out in the broad Atlantic, so far north in late spring, Brown and many others were reminded of winter in the deep South. It must have seemed as though he had been transported into an alien world very different from his humid and bloody days aboard CSS *Arkansas* and aboard *Florida* cruising the Caribbean Sea and the waters off Cape São Roque.

Brown moved forward, holding tightly to the lifelines led fore and aft, and rallied the men for yet another sail maneuver. Again, the best of the topmen scrambled aloft, already exhausted from their work just a few short hours ago. As before, they succeeded in taking the sail in. The reduction of canvas steadied the ship, slowing her progress markedly and giving the men at the wheel much better control. Instead of surging through the crests, with every possibility of broaching to, she seemed to come into harmony with them. They rose up astern, at times achieving frightening heights, and she climbed the faces, perched on the summits, affording the lookouts a spectacular view of the angry seascape, and eased down the backs of the waves with a grace and beauty sufficient to inspire admiration from the landsmen among the more seasoned tars.

The wind gradually shifted to a northerly quarter as the day wore on, clocking round almost ninety degrees. The shift granted Read the opportunity to come about and put the ship on a more northwesterly heading to hold station close-hauled in the teeth of the gale. All hands mustered on deck and smartly tacked the bark, bringing the wind hard on the starboard bow. She pitched violently into the long, sweeping crests. Water flooded the weather deck, and often submerged the sailors up to their hips.

It was tough going, but exhilarating to Read, who had been fascinated with the sea since he was a teenager in Jackson, Mississippi. With the wind and salt spray in his face as a young cadet aboard the U.S. Navy's training ship *Plymouth*, he had discovered a part of himself that had lain dormant in the backwater towns along the Yazoo River in which he spent his boyhood. As he pressed *Tacony* hard, all the skills he had acquired from his U.S. Navy service came into full play, and he was as content with his lot in life as he ever had been. He had his own ship underfoot, and a crew at his discretion to do with as he pleased.

The gale increased and the seas built

throughout the day. The wind backed from the northeast to the northwest and came in with a fury. Read ordered the topsails double reefed. *Tacony* changed course to sail by the wind, and pounded to windward with her topsails, foresail, jib, and spanker set, all the canvas he dared keep flying. The ship had been leaking since they took her from Captain Mundy, and nearly every day since Read's logbook contained the simple statement: "Pumps attended to." As the storm intensified, *Tacony* made water at a "moderate" rate, requiring the crew to man the pumps every four hours. She was a fast sailer, but her Boston owners, true to the famous Yankee thrift, evidently had not seen fit to overhaul her in recent times. As the timbers worked, the seams between her hull planking opened, and while it was normal for a wooden vessel to take on water in a heavy seaway it was nevertheless one more factor demanding Read's attention.

The men were mindful of the risks their captain was asking them to take. He had said himself when he mustered them aft on the weather deck as *Tacony* sailed away, the brig *Clarence* and the schooner *Shindler* aflame astern, that all of them should expect to be taken prisoner; that he proceeded to sail due east for several days mitigated their fear. The most dull-witted among them knew that the farther offshore they went, having recrossed the Gulf Stream, the more likely they would find shelter in the open Atlantic and elude the ships that were searching for them. The sudden turn back to the west, at the height of a storm, did not strike most of them as dangerous. Drayton thought otherwise. He was aware that they were not just hunters, but the hunted as well, and as he did on many occasions he questioned Read's wisdom.

At about 2 we tacked ship and I expect that we shall try to meet Fl. [Florida]. At any rate they [the crew] appear to give up all fear of capture. Shows what sense they have got. For the last two or three days we ran no risk and from this time hence we do, especially if we follow the course we are now steering.

The record does not show whether Read at this time had given up all hope of meeting *Florida*. His subsequent actions put him in exactly the right place at exactly the right time to rendezvous with her, as he had discussed with Maffitt. It is therefore probable that he at least considered it worth a try to keep his appointment with Maffitt. The record does show that Read's men clung to the hope that *Florida* would soon appear. Some of them found Read's mode of command objectionable and wished to return to *Florida,* and others even wished a Yankee gunboat would capture them to put an end to the voyage. These sailors, however, appear to have been in the minority. Even Drayton, despite his dislike of Read and his qualms about his management, had come to support their mission. With every additional Union merchantman they sank, the number of discontented crewmen dropped, until they to a man became completely caught up in their gleeful exercise of destruction.

None aboard *Tacony* could know that on the very day they shivered with the cold of a late spring norther, *Florida* was thousands of miles away still hunting ships above the equator off the coast of Brazil. None of them could know that Maffitt would soon turn north to commence a raid on the coast of New England, as he had told Read he would the day they parted on May 6, and that the alarm raised up and down the coast by *Tacony*'s attacks would ultimately turn *Florida* back on July 8, when she was just 50 miles due east of New York. Maffitt wrote in his journal:

> By the New York papers which we received from the ship *Sunrise*, I became aware of the fact that Lieutenant Read had, from some cause, deflected from his original instructions and had proceeded with the *Clarence* [*Tacony*] to the coast of New England, and that his great success in the work of capture and destruction had caused the Federal Government to send out quite a number of cruisers in search of his vessel. Having but a small quantity of good coal on board, I did not deem it expedient to risk the *Florida* in the raid which I had anticipated. We ran within fifty miles of New York, and found that Federal cruisers lined the whole coast, and with extreme reluctance I felt it obligatory upon me to retire from that part of the ocean.

Read remained on deck throughout most of June 16, his eyes on the sails, sea, and sky. He hoped that the cloud cover might lift long enough for him to take the sun sights required to fix his position. During one of his respites below, he noted in the salt-spattered logbook, its pale blue pages stained dark from the water dripping off his goatee, that he had taken no observations. The gale continued to increase and, once again, *Tacony* labored hard, sometimes crashing into the waves with sufficient force to knock men off their feet.

At midnight, Read called all hands to wear ship and run off before the storm. He had no other choice, yet he kept all prudent sail set until daylight revealed an awe-inspiring seascape distinctly alpine in appearance. The duration of the storm, its increasing strength, and the increasing number of miles between the ship and the land, known as among sailors, came together to create seas in excess of twenty-five feet. The crew's responses to orders slowed due to fatigue, hunger, and cold. No one paid much attention to the prisoners chained below decks. There was simply too much to do, and no hot food for anyone.

Read scribbled in his logbook: "Increasing gales. Close reefed topsails, took in foresail, reefed and furled it. Took in jib and spanker. . . . At 7:00 p.m. set in thick . . . ferocious squalls. A light drizzly rain. High seas."

Tacony fought her way on through the

night. When Read thought it was safe enough to brave a beam sea he began making his northing. At the height of the storm, the waves might have capsized the ship had he set a course that exposed the sides of the hull to the powerful seas. Examining his chart in the dim light of the lamp swaying from the bulkhead beside Captain Mundy's desk, he reviewed the plots he had marked since their escape from the waters off Chesapeake Bay. The fixes denoting established positions derived from celestial navigation revealed a steady line of progress nearly due east until the storm began. The dead reckoning showed the zigs and zags, the backtracking over the same area of ocean as he tried to avoid making too much easting. Any navigator would have been pleased at the results of Read's seamanship. Over the course of the gale, he had managed to guide the ship in a sweeping arc that gave little easting while circling northward. Connecting the plots created a line shaped much like a fishhook, with the end of the hook bending back toward Nantucket. It was as if the force of nature had tried to keep him from closing the coast of New England, as it had with *Florida* back in February, when she met with a rare winter cyclone. Read had won where Maffitt had failed. Not having to rely on coal as *Florida* did proved a great advantage.

As if in capitulation to Read and his destiny, the storm abated with the coming of dawn on June 18. The wind dropped off quickly, leaving behind a confused sea. The sea state was more dangerous than the orderly procession of monster crests that rolled away from the coast to finally lose their power and become mere swells in midocean, the last evidence of the enormity of an Atlantic storm felt thousands of miles from its source. Waves toppled and crashed together, straining the masts with the violent motion. *Tacony* pitched and rolled, and the men found it difficult to walk on deck and to shake out the reefs in the sails aloft, but the wind was down, and that, everyone realized with intense relief, signaled an inevitable end to their prolonged misery.

Bedraggled, wet, and bone tired, the crew rested in their berths below the forecastle deck. They listened to the bark work her timbers, the creak and groan of the wood, the clap and clatter of blocks, and the slap of lines against the masts. In the diminished wind, its screams now gone, the sound of the waves roaring toward the ship was frightening. The noise reminded some of thunder or a waterfall, and others, who had fought on a battlefield, of distant artillery fire blending into a continuous rumble that grew louder with the approach of the enemy. The vessel staggered as tons of water washed over the deck above their heads and streamed through crevices to splash them where they lay swinging in their hammocks. Those who were thirsty were disappointed to learn that Read had put all hands, including the prisoners, on an allowance of a half gallon of fresh water a day to conserve the dwindling supply. It seemed the misery was not over after all; it had just begun anew in a different form.

Their voyage had been long. It had taken them across more than 3,500 miles of open ocean through the tropics to the raw cold of New England, depressing with its sky often hidden behind a screen of impenetrable fog or cloaked with gray clouds. The men missed their families, homes, and fields. They longed for peace and a return to their way of life, but the rebellion called for action. The mission that brought them to these waters seemed more important than ever as *Tacony* drew closer to Nantucket, a gentle southwesterly wind blowing off the port beam to speed her onward. Their instrument of war was fire, not the minie ball or bayonet. Fire. Fire to burn bright in defiance of a vicious attempt at unjust subjugation. More than 600 miles to the west, other men with similar views continued their march northward to a place of battle not yet known to any of their generals, a little town called Gettysburg, where the larger collective destiny of a nation divided ran counter to all that the men aboard *Tacony* hoped their leaders would achieve.

Chapter Fifteen

FREEDOM GRANTED

Fishing Rip, 30 Miles Southeast of Nantucket,
3:45 p.m., June 20, 1863

The incoming tide funneled through the milewide slot of relatively deep water between the arcs of submerged sand on either side of Fishing Rip. Constantly changing with the cycles of tide and storm, the banks off Nantucket radiated outward from the island like ripples in a pond after a thrown stone disturbed the smooth water. Rising from the depths to lurk just below the surface of the sea, the banks often trapped ships whose masters lost their bearings in the frequent summer fogs. Once the vessels were fast aground, the ceaseless swells broke their backs on the hard sand beneath the keels. Although it was considered a graveyard for ships, Nantucket Shoals marked a cross-roads. Merchantmen on the transatlantic run between Europe and the United States passed in the thousands over the course of a year. Mindful of their tight schedules, the captains cut close aboard the hazards to reduce mileage before turning west for the final dash to New York Harbor along the southern shore of Long Island.

This dangerous stretch of ocean was more than a turning point on a busy maritime shipping route. Like the shoals of Georges Bank and the Grand Banks of Newfoundland to the northeast, the shallows off Nantucket provided a fine habitat for fish. The rapid tidal streams carried nutrients from deep ocean and churned a mix that attracted cod, mackerel, flounder, haddock, and herring. At the head of the food chain were the men who ventured there to fish from schooners out of ports on the coasts of New York, Connecticut, Rhode Island, and Massachusetts.

Riding to her anchor at the edge of Fishing Rip, the schooner *Micawber* rolled and pitched with the swells breaking on the outer slope of Middle Rip two miles east. The bank separating the schooner from the combers acted as a natural breakwater, but the motion was nevertheless unpleasant. However, it was just part of the job, the daily routine the crew had long since accepted as integral to their ancient trade. They hailed from Noank, Connecticut, a little harbor situated at the mouth of the Mystic River at the far reaches of eastern Long Island Sound. It was a poor town without much industry other than fishing, and in that sense it typified many of the villages on the southern New England coast.

Micawber's crew had been out for several days, having experienced a bout of nasty weather that made their lot all the harder, but the fishing had been good. Fish always seemed to like it best when the weather was foul and unfit for humans. No matter the adversity, the fishermen put to sea to catch them in all seasons of the year. The cargo wedged between bricks of ice in the hold represented a significant sum to most of them. The catch would translate to money needed to feed their families, and they looked forward to getting it to market as quickly as possible.

While many entrepreneurs in the North made fortunes from the war, times were more difficult for the lower classes, the fishermen among them. With tens of thousands of the towns' young men wounded or killed or simply gone to fight in the war, those left behind found it a challenge to keep small businesses going. The enactment in March of the Conscription Act implementing the draft posed an additional threat. Those unable to pay a commutation fee or to hire a substitute to fight in their place would have to sacrifice their jobs and possibly their lives for the greater good of the nation. Many otherwise patriotic individuals considered this an injustice. They harbored a deep-seated mistrust and loathing of a government action that forced them to fight when they were inclined to stay home. Violent protests erupted in increasing number in the Midwest and Northeast. The most famous of them all would occur in New York City on July 13, 1863. Between the draft and Robert E. Lee's northward advance there was much to discuss in the taverns ashore.

For the present, the men of *Micawber* were safe from the war, removed from its reach on Nantucket Shoals, or so they thought. The day was far from over, though the sun kept inching down the sky to eventually disappear in the haze that reduced visibility to only four or five miles. Intermittent fog swept in. It came in walls of pure white vapor that spanned the horizon and rose skyward. At other times, its arrival was not so dramatic but rather a gradual constricting of the world around the schooner until all vanished except the gray, oily swells. The sound of breakers became muffled and the band of surf faded away. The men on deck hauled their trawls while others gutted and cleaned the catch, setting up a sort of production line. Clouds of seagulls hovered overhead, darting and screeching as they dove and fought for the entrails thrown overboard by the bucketful.

None of the men paid much attention to the black bark that had emerged from the fog and made way slowly toward them from the open sea beyond the shoals. She ghosted along under full sail, a rather beautiful sight considering her sharp lines. She backed her topsails well off the banks, keeping a safe distance from the breakers and the tumult of eddies and whirls in the middle of the rips. A boat put off and the men in it worked the oars with a will. In about fifteen minutes, the boat pulled alongside. *Micawber*'s crew waved and welcomed them, thinking the visitors were interested in purchasing fish. A newspaper report published several days later questioned why the fishermen did not fight the rebels or run from them. The writer, however, offered a plausible explanation:

The question is asked why don't the fishermen fight, or run away? The cod fishermen lie at their anchors, and cannot heave them up without consuming time. The mackerel catchers are often enveloped in thick fog while fishing; in which case of course their danger is unknown until too late to escape. And then they are almost always in fleets; so that if the weather is clear, the poorest sailers may be easily run down.

As to fighting, they have no weapons more deadly than their bait knives, which are not of long range. One of the men captured on Fishing Rip, informs us that the *Tacony* hove in sight on the lifting up of a fog bank, and a boat was seen coming towards the schooner he was in. It being a common thing for large vessels in passing to send their boats to purchase fresh fish, no particular notice was taken of the bark or boat. The fishermen did not even leave their lines until the pirates rushed across the deck, and presented cocked pistols at their heads.

The *Micawber*'s crew stared at the group of sailors, none of whom wore the uniform of the Confederacy. The surprise was complete. They were lined up on deck at gunpoint and told not to move or they would be shot. The officer in charge went below and appeared a few minutes later with the vessel's charts, logbook, and sextant. There was nothing else of value for him to take.

"You are prisoners of the Confederate States of America," the man said. He then ordered the crew into their two dories.

The fishermen hesitated. The captain objected, asked why he should obey. But it was no use. The rebel sailors were already preparing to burn the schooner. They piled bedding, rags, small stuff (rope yarns), and other combustibles on deck, covered them with the tar used to protect the standing rigging, and poured on sperm-whale oil from the lamps and turpentine from the paint locker. Rebels working below made similar arrangements to fire the schooner. When all was ready, and everyone but the arson team had evacuated the vessel, they set her ablaze.

Micawber's crew rowed slowly toward the bark. The rebel officer seated in the stern of the boat abreast of them aimed a pistol in their direction to prevent their escape. It was clear that any effort to row away would result in the deaths of most, if not all, of the schooner's crew, though the idea to try it likely crossed their minds. *Micawber's* master thought of another solution, a compromise, and he hoped the rebel commander might consider it. He shouted over to the boarding officer asking to address his captain, and the man agreed to make it so. The two boats from the schooner and the one with the rebel boarding party skirted the white water at the edge of the rips and came to rest a short distance off the bark's stern. Written in gold across the transom was her name, *Tacony*. A small man wearing an oversized peacoat stood at the taffrail, his hands clasped behind his back. He looked down at them, his face expressionless.

"The schooner's skipper wants to talk with you, sir," the boarding officer said, and took his boat alongside, where men prepared to haul it back on deck.

Read listened to the Yankee schoonerman's request to remain in the boats and make for shore rather than submit to being taken prisoner. Based on what he had observed of these shoal waters, it seemed a risky proposition to row through the rips and breakers to head for land that lay almost forty miles to the northwest — a full day of hard work at the oars, no doubt. With no food or water, and no compass, the journey would test the hardiest of fellows and the best of seamen. If the weather turned bad, they might not reach safe harbor, yet he understood why they would want to attempt it. He was prepared himself to do all he might to avoid ending up as a prisoner, including fighting against superior odds as long as a chance existed to elude his pursuers. In that sense, these Yanks were like him and his men. They prized their freedom and dignity as much as he did.

Several hours earlier, off Phelps Bank eleven miles to the southeast, *Tacony* had overhauled the American packet *Isaac Webb* of the Black Ball Line, the oldest transatlantic shipping company in the United States. She was inbound from Liverpool to New York with 750 passengers. He had wanted to burn her but could not because he had no place to put the ship's people. He instead bonded her for $40,000 and sent her on her way, along with the prisoners taken off the brig *Umpire* that he had captured and burned on June 15. Provisions and water were in short supply, and he was unable to procure anything from *Isaac Webb*. He was certain to snare additional vessels in these busy waters, and the more room he had aboard *Tacony*

274

for prisoners the better. In the meantime, food and water would last longer if he allowed these schoonermen to brave the sea in their small boats, as they desired.

"You may go," Read said.

Micawber's crew turned their boats to the northwest and rowed quickly back toward the shoals. As they neared Middle Rip, another fog bank swept in. They watched *Tacony* fill away on a northerly heading to run up the outer edge of the shallows in deep water. Her form became indistinct, her long black hull a dark slash in contrast to the light mist. The yellowish hue of her canvas faded first and soon she merged with the surrounding vapor and disappeared from sight altogether, but her presence lingered. It manifested itself in the crackle, hiss, and roar of the flames enveloping *Micawber*. The men worked the oars to hold station against the tide. For a long moment they kept the sterns of the dories pointed at the burning schooner that had seen them through many a storm and provided a means to earn a living. For some, the spectacle must have been terribly sad. For others, it must have instilled in them a profound hatred of the rebels.

As they watched, the schooner broke free from her anchor, the wooden bitts at the bow burned through, along with the heavy iron ring mounted below to secure the bitter end of the rode. The rode splashed into the sea. The current caught her and twirled her around in a slow, fiery dance, and she drifted toward the breakers on the west side of Fishing Rip. In moments, she plunged into the confused waters, and as she pitched violently in the maelstrom her masts crashed down and tore away. The flames soared high, engulfing her completely. She moved fast and entered a thick swirl of fog. Only the orange glow distinguished her form, like a sun or star fallen to the surface of the gray ocean. The mist reflected the light and softened it, making the scene almost beautiful.

The captain said, "We better get moving." And the long row began.

The crew, numbering eight to ten men, rowed steadily and with power, exerting themselves in a routine that came naturally from years of service on the banks. Their hands were callused and rough, their backs, shoulders, and arms strong. They knew these waters better than most people know the streets of their hometowns, and although they understood the risks, they welcomed their freedom and thanked God for it. To have been taken prisoner was a dishonor, a calamity to add injury to the loss they had already endured.

The sun was invisible. Yet its light through the fog and haze shone with greater intensity to the west than it did to the east. The swells rolling in from the storm of the past several days headed eastward. They steered by the sun until it set and in the darkness they kept the boats' bows to the swells to guide them onward over the deep cuts through the shoals. When the seas broke in confusion, the motion told them they had strayed from their course. They backtracked and tried again, heading for Davis Bank. They improvised a lead line, a device used to sound the depths to determine how deep the water was beneath the boats. Their soundings provided additional clues to their position. They stayed close together, for there was safety in numbers. Though they could see nothing in the pitch black of the foggy, cold night, they maintained their close distance through the rhythmic splash as the blades dipped deep and the grind of the oars against the gunwales and the thole pins used to secure them.

The men tired as the hours wore on, but they kept rowing, hopeful that the ordeal might soon end. They had told the captain of the rebel bark they would row for Nantucket nearly forty miles to the northwest, a logical course of action for all unfamiliar with these waters. They gambled that the man knew nothing of the small light vessel anchored over Old South Shoal, about ten miles southeast of the island, and about twenty-two miles east-southeast of Fishing Rip. The beacon warned the coastwise traffic of a patch of shallows little more than ten feet deep, less in some spots, and potentially lethal even in calm conditions because of the breakers that made out from the area in all directions. They counted on the loom of the light to guide them to safety.

Tension mounted among the men when the beacon did not appear at the appointed time. The tide had turned. If they failed to row hard to counter the stream, it might carry them back out to sea where they would almost certainly die of thirst, starvation, or exposure. It might also carry them into the maze of dangerous shoals that claimed the lives of even the most experienced seamen who found themselves at the mercy of the sea as it clashed with the sand banks. The night stretched into a seeming eternity. The men rowed in shifts. Those off duty shivered in the cold water sloshing in the bottom of the boats, heavy with the odor of fish and slick with slime. Approximately eight hours after setting out, the first indication of the light vessel appeared as two pricks of white in the darkness — the illumination from the lanterns mounted at the trucks of the ship's masts. The spirits of the men improved and they rowed with renewed vigor.

The shouts of *Micawber*'s men startled the lookout standing watch on the South Shoal Light Ship. He did not expect a hail in the middle of nowhere in the depths of night. He rushed to the side of the vessel and peered down at the water, but could see nothing of the men crying for help until they reached the side of the ship. Thinking they were castaways, he hurried to deploy a Jacob's ladder to enable them to climb aboard. The entire crew of the light vessel listened to their tale. A rebel! So far north! News of a raider off the Carolinas had broken on June 12, and that of the raid off the Chesapeake on June 14. No further word of the pirate had appeared in the newspapers, save for reports of frantic activity at Navy yards up and down the coast as orders flowed in from Washington to charter, seize, or purchase every available ship or yacht capable of fighting the deadly interloper.

The main emphasis in the press at this time was on Lee's march into Union territory. However, the fact that at least one commerce raider was attacking merchant ships off the coast in Union waters was seen as a double threat, and there were rumors that more than one rebel "pirate" was at large. In the Thursday, June 18 edition of the *Eastern Argus*, a newspaper serving Portland, Maine, the editor reprinted a long editorial published in the *New York Times* commenting on the confusion both the land and sea invasions were causing in the War and Navy Departments.

It is the withholding of the news of rebel movements, that does more than anything else to precipitate the country into demoralizing excitements. We were assured last week, up to the very last day, that the rebel army was still at Fredericksburg — while the fact is, that they must have begun their march with the week, for on Friday they appeared before Winchester, in the Shenandoah Valley. . . . It is disgraceful that a great nation should thus appear as poltroons in presence of a rebel army which it ought to be able to devour body and boots. One such scare would be bad enough, but in two years we have had half a dozen. If ever we get over this one, it will doubtless be repeated in about four months.

We have now a double panic — one for sea and one for land; the privateers are on our coast and Lee is in Pennsylvania. The rebels laugh at these panics of ours; they themselves seem never to indulge in them. Foreign nations laugh at them, and sneer at us. . . . If the Government, instead of treating the people as children, would treat them as intelligent citizens, we should not so often disgrace country and ourselves by these panics.

It appeared that these fishermen were the first to encounter the rebels since June 14 and possessed vital information for the Navy Department. That "double threat" alluded to in the *New York Times* was now more than just a rumor; it was reality. In the morning, the lightship signaled to the passing schooner *Antietam*, outbound for Georges Banks. Nevertheless, *Micawber*'s crew transferred to her, hoping to meet an inbound vessel in short order. The waters off Nantucket were crowded with fishing craft. It was a reasonable expectation, and sure enough, the men were soon put aboard the schooner *Eastern Star*, bound for Martha's Vineyard. The news report of their encounter with *Tacony*, published in the June 25 edition of the *New York Times*, indicated that crewman S. Moses arrived at Edgartown, Martha's Vineyard, on June 23, at which time the news of the rebels in New England waters began to send shock waves throughout the fishing community.

It was already too late for the clipper ship *Byzantium*. She sailed straight toward *Tacony* only ten miles from Fishing Rip, her master forewarned of a Confederate raider headed north but whose whereabouts were unknown. He had received the news from Commander A. S. Baldwin, captain of the chartered steamer *Blackstone*, searching the waters for *Tacony* "between the western edge of the Gulf Stream and the shoals of Nantucket and the two Georges to the eastward as far as longitude 62 degrees West and north to latitude 42 degrees."

Tacony cruised in precisely this area of ocean, destroying *Byzantium* and the bark *Goodspeed*, as the men of *Micawber* sailed toward safe harbor. Many miles to the west, off the southern shore of Long Island, the packet *Isaac Webb* heeled to a gentle breeze just one day out of New York. She arrived on June 22, with tidings of the Confederate cruiser and her latest location; the newspapers published the story of her meeting with *Tacony* on June 23. The bad news of *Tacony*'s appearance in New England waters prompted the owners of Nesmith & Sons to write in frustration to Gideon Welles about the apparent inept conduct of the U.S. Navy. They suggested that the U.S. government put a price on the pirates' heads, that such a measure might at last lead to their speedy capture. "Would it not answer a better purpose than anything that has yet been done? As matters stand now, our glorious flag is gradually disappearing from the ocean, either by destruction or the large war insurance, obliging the sale of our ships to foreigners."

The men of *Micawber* added their voices to the growing number of victims calling on the U.S. Navy to defend American commerce as zealously as it enforced the blockade. Panic began to increase with this latest spate of news, both about Lee and *Tacony*. Volunteer militia patrolled the beaches along the Massachusetts shore. Watchers scanned the sea for signs of the pirate. Cries for the Army to send guns for the protection of the towns poured into the War Department, and there were requests for troops as well. But there were no troops to send. They were all massing in Pennsylvania to stop Lee's men.

Neither Lee nor Read was panicking. On the contrary, both men, one a great general commanding a formidable army, the other an inexperienced leader of less than two dozen men, redoubled their efforts to carry out their respective missions.

Chapter Sixteen

CRIES OF OUTRAGE

Washington, D.C., Navy Department, June 24, 1863

The chief clerk handed Gideon Welles yet another dispatch concerning *Tacony*. The little cruiser, alone and without heavy guns, had succeeded in stirring up fright along the coast from Delaware to Maine, and Welles's displeasure increased. He saw no reason to overreact, but others were less able than he to maintain a cool, calm approach to the disturbing events. *Tacony*'s captain appeared bent on burning any vessel he ran across that flew the Stars and Stripes. From a large ship to a lowly schooner, it did not seem to matter much to him, as long as the craft was Yankee. The indiscriminate mayhem was distasteful to Welles, and indicated a wanton disregard of all moral precepts governing the conduct of war.

The impact of these raids Welles at first dismissed as a short-lived inconvenience. As time passed and the rebels remained at large, it became obvious that, although many merchants and officials from local and state governments were wrong in ascribing an apocalyptic magnitude to the destruction, the doings of the pirates did appear to merit further action. Word of the detention and bonding of the packet *Isaac Webb* on June 20 and additional news of *Tacony*'s ravages that followed bolstered Welles's desire to see the rebels caught as soon as possible. At least nine more vessels had been destroyed in the last three days right in the main path of the transatlantic shipping lanes, and embarrassingly enough, right in the middle of a dragnet of U.S. cruisers. The newspaper reporters, of course, would point this out, and did so with sarcasm as evidenced by the following report from the *New York Times* published on June 26:

The *Tacony*. — If to no one else, it will be a matter of delight to Secretary Welles to learn that a large United States steamer was seen cruising off Chatham on Wednesday last [June 24]. Only a couple of days previous the rebel brig *Tacony* had committed a series of daring depredations in that vicinity. With a celerity that could hardly have been expected, the Secretary of the Navy succeeded in getting a cruiser to the spot just two days after the pestiferous little craft had taken her departure. The large United States steamer will doubtless enjoy the soft Summer breezes of her new cruising ground, but we doubt if the pirate will be much disturbed by her presence. The most remarkable results may be anticipated from locking the safe after the spoons have been stolen. There is, of course, a strong probability that the robbers will continue to hover round the place.

If the status quo held, the costs of the rebel incursion into the home waters of the Union would rise. The expenses involved in personnel, charter fees, vessel purchases, coal, losses for cargoes and ships, and soaring insurance were indeed quite significant already. With this in mind, Welles scanned the terse, plaintive telegram sent at 9:20 a.m. from the Boston mercantile company of A. Hardy & Co. and received shortly thereafter at the Navy Department. The owners wanted guns from the Navy yard at Charlestown to arm private vessels, which they intended to send after *Tacony* at their own expense. Implicit in the letter was an understated conviction that the Navy was incapable, or at best ineffectual, in its efforts to hunt the pirates down and bring them to justice. Much of Welles's burgeoning irritation about the entire matter stemmed from such correspondence, for it cast his department in a poor light, and thus reflected badly on him. It also exposed him to attack from his critics in Congress and those in the cabinet who disliked him, and delighted in anything that made him twitch with discomfort.

The Bostonians offered a $10,000 bounty for the capture of the pirates, and now they wanted him to arm private ships to facilitate the chase. It struck him as all too similar to issuing letters of marque, a tactic he was still not willing to support, given its potential adverse implications for foreign relations. However, under the present circumstances, he decided to approve the company's request, provided that the officers selected to take command of any private vessels engaged in the pursuit of *Tacony* were officially appointed as acting volunteers for the Navy and subject to its code of conduct. As long as the men were affiliated with the Navy, and acted in accordance with its rules of engagement, the United States would not open itself up to any of the transgressions against neutral vessels that had almost touched off a war with England on so many previous occasions. At least it decreased the odds of unforeseen consequences that reached beyond the mere hunt for a lone raider.

Welles called a clerk in and explained his intentions. The clerk left and returned shortly with drafts of telegrams for A. Hardy & Co. and Commodore J. B. Montgomery, Commandant of the Navy Yard at Charlestown. Welles looked them over, checking to make sure all the basic details were included in the text. The short message to Montgomery appeared to cover every important contingency:

Messrs. A. Hardy & Co., of Boston, wish to send out some vessels after the *Tacony*, and you are hereby authorized to furnish said vessels with arms; and such officers as they recommend to serve on board you will appoint according to the rules of the service for this special service without pay.

Earlier in the morning, Welles sent word

to his senior officers at Hampton Roads, Philadelphia, and New York reporting *Tacony*'s last known position on Georges Bank, roughly one hundred twenty miles east of Nantucket. To Acting Rear Admiral S. P. Lee, Commander of the North Atlantic Blockading Squadron in Hampton Roads, he also ordered the information conveyed to the captain of USS *Tuscarora*, which was about to sail in search of the rebels. Likewise, he instructed Rear Admiral Hiram Paulding, Commandant of the New York Navy Yard, to send the USS *San Jacinto* and "any other available vessels in search of the *Tacony*," and instructed any ships just arrived back in Philadelphia to immediately proceed to sea again to search for her off Georges Bank.

The instructions given to the individual masters of the search vessels ordered a thorough canvass of the waters from New York to Cape Sable, Nova Scotia, and beyond to the Grand Banks of Newfoundland. These captains were advised that they might, if they considered it effective, sail under false colors to lure the rebels into range of their guns, and some of them did just that, though with negative results. The Navy knew of *Tacony*'s approximate position, but Welles and assistant Fox could not be sure that the rebels would stay in one place for long. *Tacony*'s captain was too smart to make such a stupid mistake, requiring Welles to order a broader search area that thinned the dragnet.

There was also the very distinct possibility that the rebels might hop to another ship. The lag time between the discovery of the switch and the conveyance of the news to the searchers might extend from several days to over a week. In the meantime, the rebels could continue their cruise with substantially less risk of capture. So, the imperative at the moment was to catch the pirates before they escaped or shifted to another captured vessel. Welles jotted down the following short message to Commodore Montgomery in Boston, the second one of the day: "Charter more steamers and send them after the *Tacony*; all that can be sent in forty-eight hours." A clerk hurried off to the telegraph office with it.

The political ramifications of the raider's destruction of New England shipping were not lost on Welles. For quite some time, the governor of Massachusetts, John A. Andrew, had been pressuring him to send cruisers and ironclads to patrol the coastal waters and defend the harbors in response to the depredations of *Florida* and *Alabama*. With a raider off the New England coast confirmed, the man would no doubt bring further pressure to bear. Foreseeing this, Welles sent Andrew a short telegram, advising him that he authorized the arming of private ships and the deployment of additional vessels to hunt for *Tacony*. He wisely provided the governor with written proof that he was doing his utmost to rid the sea of this young upstart from the South. He also established a paper trail he might point to if an investigation ensued regarding the conduct of the Navy and himself in the matter.

These telegrams were the latest in a series of correspondence to reach Welles regarding *Tacony*'s depredations. It came in like the tide in the Bay of Fundy, sweeping across his desk without the least prospect of slackening until Read was captured. Pleas from New York for ironclads and the frigate *Roanoke* to protect the harbor, and other requests from smaller towns along the coast, he considered and denied for lack of resources. More than twenty ships were hunting for the rebel; the number would expand to almost forty in the coming days. He could spare none to remain idle in harbor. It appeared likely that the raider would not venture near a well-protected city, but rather stay at sea where it was easier to hide, thereby justifying his inclination to keep the cruisers offshore instead of on duty in port.

Welles remained focused throughout the day on the hunt for *Tacony*. He reviewed all the naval assets that might be available, leaving none unconsidered. He sent additional telegrams to Hiram Paulding in New York and Commodore C. K. Stribling in Philadelphia. He asked the former for the charter of the steamship *Ericsson*, and queried the latter as to whether *Shenandoah* might be sent east to reinforce the warships patrolling New England waters. At 3:40 p.m., a clerk dropped a telegram from Montgomery on Welles's desk.

Telegram received. Search for the steamers now in progress. U.S. steamers *Howquah* and *Iron Age* will be dispatched within twenty-four hours, unless otherwise ordered.

And at 4:05 p.m., Welles received a response from Paulding sent through one of the officer's subordinates.

Received your telegram. Have sent the

San Jacinto after the *Tacony*. Will send such other vessels as I can get.

Welles stayed late at the Navy Department. The sun was long down when he took his leave and walked slowly across Lafayette Square to his home. The air was thick with the humidity draped over the uneasy city like a heavy coat, suffocating in its effect. The summer just begun was one of the hottest in recent memory. Sweat caused Welles's clothes to cling to his skin, and his scalp itched under his wig. The layers of his beard were damp. The hairs at the bottom over his chest were actually wet as the moisture wicked downward. He longed for the cool sea breezes on the shores of Connecticut in late June. He remembered the happier days he had spent in Hartford with Mary shortly after their marriage in 1835, when he finished his lengthy and rewarding tenure as editor of the *Hartford Times*, and soon thereafter became postmaster of Hartford. That first year of marriage had been one of the brightest in Welles's life.

Once home, Welles ate a small supper and sequestered himself in his study after exchanging pleasantries with Mary, as he had done habitually almost every day since his early twenties while studying law in Hartford. His study had always been his haven, a place where the world did not intrude and where he was able to contemplate its vagaries. It was during the quiet hours that he caught up on personal correspondence and wrote in his journals. On this particular night, he was concerned with the obvious matter of Robert E. Lee's invasion and the frustration he felt at the lack of communication from the War Department regarding Hooker's moves to thwart it.

No definite or satisfactory information in regard to military movements. If it were clear that the Secretary of War and General-in-Chief knew and were directing military movements intelligently, it would be a relief; but they communicate nothing and really appear to have little or nothing to communicate. What at any time surprises us, surprises them.

Also at the forefront of his thoughts during those hours alone, the clock ticking nearby and the occasional sound of traffic on H Street carrying to him in the room, was the terminal illness of his long-time friend, Admiral Andrew H. Foote. Welles had met the younger Foote at the age of seventeen during his short-lived studies at the Cheshire Academy in Cheshire, Connecticut, about a day's ride from his hometown of Glastonbury. His nimble mind and formidable memory enabled Welles to master his studies at the local school with little effort, and he became listless and bored. The death of his brother, Samuel, who drowned in the spring of 1818, preceded by the deaths of his grandparents and his mother in relatively quick succession, caused him to draw inward. He spent most of his time on solitary walks and in the cemetery, the graves of his loved ones his only companions. Fearing for his child's welfare, Welles's father sent him to Cheshire, hoping it might provide him with an opportunity to find peace with himself, cultivate his social skills, and acquire an education. Welles encountered the same problems at Cheshire that he did in his hometown, but the friendship he developed with Foote was one of the more lasting virtues of his two years there.

Now, forty-four years after their first meeting, Welles's friend lay dying in a room at the Astor House in New York City. His condition had declined in the last few days and his prognosis for recovery appeared uncertain at best. It was thought that a wound he had sustained in the battle for Fort Donelson on the Cumberland River in February 1862, a followup to his victory with a flotilla of ironclads at Fort Henry, contributed to his current ill health, but Welles considered it just a part of the equation. Foote's untiring work in the early days of the war on the river campaign to gain control of the upper reaches of the Mississippi had sapped his strength. The climate did not agree with Foote, and the stress of the assignment took its toll. His health had never really rebounded afterward.

The record does not indicate it, but it appears likely that Welles must have entertained the notion that he was partially responsible for Foote's illness, albeit indirectly. In spite of his friend's precarious health, he had appointed Foote to take over the South Atlantic Blockading Squadron from Admiral Du Pont, whom Welles relieved from duty, in large part due to his lackluster performance at Charleston. In Welles's estimation, Foote was the most appropriate officer for the command, and his friend welcomed the opportunity to serve. The personal risks involved were shelved in favor of the greater importance of winning the war. Foote was just about ready to depart for duty when he became bedridden and soon lapsed into a state of near death. Welles's diary entries for the latter part of June were filled with references to his close friendship with Foote and his grief upon hearing the news of his death on June 26.

A telegram last night informed me of the death of Admiral Foote. The information of the last few days made it a not unexpected event, yet there was a shock when it came. Foote and myself were schoolboys together at Cheshire Academy under good old Dr. Bronson, and, though three or four years younger than myself, we were pursuing some of the same studies, and there then sprang up an attachment between us that never was broken. . . . When I was called to take the administration of the Navy Department, he was Executive Officer at the Brooklyn Navy Yard, and wrote me of the pleasure my appointment gave him. . . .

Towards me he exhibited a deference that was to me, who wished a revival and continuance of the friendly and social intimacy of earlier years, often painful. But the discipline of the sailor would not permit him to do differently, and when I once or twice spoke of it, he insisted it was proper, and said it was a sentiment which he felt even in our schoolday intercourse and friendship.

Welles was also worried about Lee's invasion, was disgusted with the War Department, and unsure of Hooker's ability to lead the Army of the Potomac to victory. The rebel pirate was taking on more importance as the days passed and the Navy failed to capture him. He expressed his irritation over how his handling of recent events was likely to be portrayed in the public view. Welles was, and always had been, deeply ambitious and mindful of the capricious ways of the voters, and cognizant of the damage even the appearance of ineffectiveness might do to an otherwise respectable career in government.

None of our vessels have succeeded in capturing the Rebel pirate Tacony, which has committed great ravages along the coast, although I have sent out over twenty vessels in search. Had she been promptly taken, I should have been blamed for such a needless and expensive waste of strength; now I shall be censured for not doing more.

Welles was correct in his predictions. Salvos of criticism were headed his way. The next several days were to prove more vexing than ever. All Welles could do was direct his forces with the information at hand, which was precious little, and hope that the young rebel commander might finally make a fatal mistake.

Chapter Seventeen

DESPERATE DECEPTION

At Sea, Ninety Miles Southwest of Cape Sable, 1:00 a.m., June 25, 1863

The darkness was almost complete over the waters just south of the Bay of Fundy. The orange moon, which had earlier risen over the horizon and gradually lost its peculiar peach color as the hours passed, had set not long since. Its presence in the sky, intermittently obscured with the passage of jagged clouds, served the men of *Tacony* well in their current labors, illuminating the sea in a pale shimmer while the boat crews plied between the bark and the fishing schooner *Archer* hove to in the light, warm breeze. With the moon gone, the men relied on the yellow flicker of the lanterns brought on deck and the dim light of the stars visible during breaks in the cloud cover. The sound of oars splashing through the freezing water, the suck and whoosh along the waterlines of the vessels as they rolled to the swells, and the hurried urgent tones of the low voices of the Confederates punctuated the otherwise quiet repose of the ocean in the small hours of the morning.

The men fought their fatigue. None had slept much during the previous few days leading up to the desperate move to abandon their fine, swift bark. The demands of the mission precluded eating and resting in peace. As *Tacony* made her way northeastward, up the outer edge of the New England coast through foggy, dank weather that wormed a chill deep in the bones of the Southerners, she left in her wake the blazing wrecks of seven schooners and two ships, with two other large merchantmen and a small fishing smack released after their masters pledged bonds.

On June 22 alone, four of the fishing craft were set afire — *Marengo*, *Elizabeth Ann*, *Rufus Choate*, and *Ripple*. The rebels herded the crews aboard a fifth schooner, *Florence*, deemed too old for the torch, and much needed as a transport for the captured fishermen. They were sent away with the sailors of the bark *Goodspeed* and the clipper ship *Byzantium*, save for three of the roughest serving aboard the clipper.

These hardened tars hailed from New Orleans and had chosen to enlist with Read. They seized an opportunity to double their wages of twelve to fifteen dollars per month, and the money was to be paid in gold, of which Read had plenty stuffed in his carpet bag along with the bonds, ship's papers, and other documents collected during the cruise. In addition, 25 percent of the total take in prizes was allocated for the officers and crew, to be paid out in twentieths, according to rank and position at war's end and upon the Confederacy's receipt of the payments promised in the bonds. For sailors to switch sides was not uncommon. If more money could be made on another ship, that made all the difference. Loyalty to a cause or a nation did not matter.

The burning fishing smacks shone like beacons in the fog as the bark filled away, leaving the Yankee schooner with her seventy-five frightened and angry men to make their way to safe harbor and report the latest news of the piratical depredations occurring so close to shore. The raider gradually disappeared in the twilight, her navigation lights unlit to assure stealth. "We concluded the day by capturing some more fishermen. . . . We move off with a light breeze by the light of three burning schooners," Drayton wrote.

The destruction of property was the sole aim of the raider, and burning or bonding large merchant ships the focus of attention. The rebels viewed the decimation of so many fishing craft with some ambivalence, though their minor qualms failed to deter them. There was no room for mercy in war, but even Read found sinking humble fishing vessels a sour task. He told several of the masters, as later reported by them in the press, that he regretted the necessity of burning their schooners, saying he did so from a sense of duty to the Confederacy. Drayton recorded similar sentiments in his diary on June 23, when *Tacony*'s crew sacked and burned two more schooners on Georges Banks, acknowledging the disastrous financial consequences for the people with his typical sprinkle of spite:

About 9:00 a.m. made another fisher. Boarded him and burnt her. She is Ada of Gloucester and the Captain, the owner, worked for twelve years to get her. He and those belonging to him will now feel the effects of war at their own doors and in their families as well as we do. . . . [We burned] the schooner Wanderer, a fisher. The Capt. like the other had just cleared her after working 30 years through snows and all kinds of weather. It is hard but honest as the saying goes.

The prevailing view of the rebels was that while they had done damage to the Yankees, it amounted to "not one tenth what they have done to us" and that the mission indeed had been achieving the effect of "hitting them in their tenderest spot, viz, their pocketbooks."

Throughout June 24, as *Tacony* approached the tip of Nova Scotia, Read engaged in a showdown with the master of the ship *Shatemuc*, bound to Boston from Liverpool. Having brought her to with the last of his ammunition for the howitzer, he discovered she carried approximately three hundred fifty immigrants and a cargo of iron plate he believed was intended for use in Union shipyards employed in the construction of ironclads. The master refused to accept terms for bonding and said he preferred the rebels burn the ship, likely aware that the Southern captain could not do so unless he found a means to transfer the ship's company to other vessels. With a boarding party left aboard *Shatemuc*, the crew of which seemed ready at any moment to resist and cause unnecessary bloodshed, Read set off with *Tacony* to chase down every vessel in sight, overhauling two, which proved to be British and whose captains refused to accept prisoners.

Frustrated, Read returned to *Shatemuc* hours later for a polite but firm conversation with her master. At last, seeing the situation was in stalemate, the captain relented and pledged the prodigious bond of $150,000. He took the prisoners from *Ada* and *Wanderer*, and went on his way. Soon thereafter, the wind fell light, and the two ships remained within sight of one another. A schooner also hove within view. Believing she was a Yankee, Read ordered an armed boat crew to row several miles to her. In the deepening twilight, and with the commencement of a light breeze, the boarding party sailed back to *Tacony* with their prize, the captured schooner *Archer*.

"Run down the *Shatemuc* and put those prisoners aboard her," Read said, and the officer obeyed.

It was dark before the rebels returned with *Archer*. She was of lighter displacement, and her fore-and-aft rig was better suited for sailing to windward. They overhauled Shatemuc and put the prisoners aboard. Upon Archer's return, Read called all hands remaining aboard *Tacony* aft. He withheld no information from his men, as he had done earlier in the voyage, and told them frankly what he intended to do. He recorded his plan on June 25, during a moment alone in the cabin previously occupied by Archer's captain.

The latest news from Yankeedom [obtained from newspapers taken from prizes] tells us that there are over 20 gunboats in search of us. They have the description of the Tacony and overhaul every vessel that resembles her. During the night we transferred all our things on board the schooner Archer. At 2:00 a.m. set fire to the Tacony and stood west. The schooner Archer is a fishing vessel of 90 tons, sails well, and is easily handled. No Yankee gunboat would even dream of suspecting us. I therefore think we will dodge our pursuers for a short time. It is my intention to go along the coast with a view of burning the shipping in some exposed harbor [and] of cutting out a steamer.

Thus, with the transfer complete and the fires lit, the men aboard *Archer* sailed away from the ship that had been so useful to them. Like all the others, she made a beautiful and yet forlorn scene as the flames reduced her to a hulk, her hull distinguished as a slender band atop the dark sea, the fire leaping high. Some of the men stood on the deck and watched her drop astern, until the site of her destruction was a mere glow in the night. Others lay down on coils of rope, on their duffels, anywhere a bit of comfort might be found, and sank immediately into a deep sleep. Drayton was among the latter.

As soon as I got aboard the Archer it seemed like coming from a large house into a very small one. Everything crowded and in a dire confusion. Tired and awful sleepy not having but little sleep the night before. Dropped myself wherever I could and was asleep immediately.

The men off watch awoke to a bright, clear day. A fresh breeze from the southwest blew hard on the schooner's port bow. She carried full sail, the sheets hauled in tight to give her sufficient lift and power to push through the whitecaps. Her lee rail dipped low, and water and foam bubbled through the scuppers at the bases of the bulwarks to wash the deck dark with brine. The rigging hummed and the ocean seethed as the vessel made way steadily toward land. She threw sheets of spray to leeward and astern patches of white froth streamed in the wake. Read ordered the man at the helm to ease her a bit. Sailing west-northwest on a close reach, she picked up speed.

"Our new vessel sails like the wind," Drayton wrote, though he also complained about the jerky motion of the schooner; it made him feel seasick. It was quite a transition for him and the rest of the crew to move down to a craft so much smaller than *Tacony*, but they all looked forward to the prospect of having her for only a few days. They expected to find something faster.

During the next twenty-four hours, *Archer* ticked off a fine run of 110 miles across the mouth of the Bay of Fundy, her bow pointed straight toward the heart of the Maine coast. The lookout aloft on the forenoon watch the morning of June 26 cried out, "Land ho!" Off in the distance to starboard, a deep-blue clump loomed above the ocean, the high cliffs of Monhegan Island, one of the larger projections of granite that bejewel the midcoast region of Maine. A landmark for sailors over the centuries, it represented the first sight of land for the rebel crew since April, when they cruised aboard *Florida* near Brazil.

For any sailor, making landfall after months at sea teases out emotions filled with excitement and longing for imminent relief from the constant motion of the vessel, the hard work, and the occasional danger that marks life under sail. It was no different for Read's men, in spite of the fact that this was enemy land. Along with the pleasant view of the coast materializing before them came a sense of unbounded pride at what they had accomplished and might soon achieve in the near future. Between June 6 and June 24, they had captured, bonded, or burned twenty-one Union merchantmen, a record that would make their leaders back in Richmond smile.

The question remained, however, as to what they would do next. Read occupied his usual position on the aft deck away from all the others aboard, and stared at the land spreading out before him in a vast panorama of whites, blues, and green set atop the sparkling sea. He contemplated his options, running through a list of harbors he knew about from studying the charts taken off the prizes. The largest city in the area was Portland, but he knew little about it other than the location. What were the defenses and how well were they manned? What prizes might lie in the harbor to make it worth the risk of an attack?

Eight miles southeast of Damariscove Island, a long, low stretch of rock covered with meadows lying well off the mainland, two fishermen hauled the trawls they had set the night before. Setting and hauling was a routine as familiar to them as the ascent and descent of the sun, the cold grasp of a Maine fog, and the sweet scent of pine carried on a warm southerly wind blown across the bays and sounds, all the more pungent in the narrow passages of water between the thousands of islands scattered along the coast like stones in a quarry. Albert T. Bibber and Elbridge Titcomb, both from the Casco Bay town of Falmouth, paid little attention to the schooner bearing down on them at a fast clip. When she rounded up, her sails luffing in the breeze, they stopped their work for a moment. A man on the stern waved and shouted, "Boat ahoy! Come alongside!"

The fishermen looked at each other, shrugged, and went back to work, ignoring the hail.

"Boat ahoy!" the man shouted again.

Read had secreted most of his sailors below under orders to remain quiet. On Archer's deck were eight or nine crewmen dressed as fishermen. Some of them were allowed to drink hard liquor and were encouraged to act drunk. It was a ruse to fool the fishermen, and it worked. Bibber and Titcomb came aboard thinking the men were "drunken fishermen on a frolic." After some conversation and the payment of twenty dollars each in gold, they agreed to pilot the schooner for their apparently inebriated peers. The vessel was put on a new heading, nearly due west, and closed with Seguin Island, a tiny speck off the mouth of the Kennebec River about twenty miles east of the outer approaches to Portland harbor.

Off Portland I picked up two fishermen, who, taking us for a pleasure party, willingly consented to pilot us into Portland. From the fishermen I learned that the revenue cutter *Caleb Cushing* was in the harbor of Portland, and the passenger steamer to New York — a stanch, swift propeller — would remain in Portland during the night. I at once determined to enter the harbor, and at night to quietly seize the cutter and steamer.

The land drew closer and its features became bold. The high cliffs on the seaward side of Seguin rose from the sea, the lighthouse clearly visible on the brow of the bluffs. Surf broke at the base of the cliffs and on submerged rocks and ledges, flashing white with the rhythm of the surge. Read brought *Archer* to within a mile and a half of Seguin, not far from the vessel's home harbor on Southport Island up the Sheepscot River, whose deep, cold waters yielded rich catches of lobster. He turned west to run offshore along the expanse of Casco Bay's fringe of outer islands. Portland Harbor lay just a few hours away. Enjoying the sail and the warm summer breeze, and anticipating with enthusiasm what the night might bring, Drayton wrote in his diary:

Would not there be some excitement in Portland now if they but knew that we were so close to them. A steamer would be out for us in a hurry. We are bound on some dare devil operation. Whatever it is I know the general impression is that we shall cut out the cutter laying in the Harbor of Portland and then take a steamer. If we are only successful we shall have some glory and have taken the sails out of some on board the Florida. As soon as they hear of our exploits, I bet they will bite their lips for I think they have fooled themselves good. So much for the rivalry and petty malice. If we were to meet her tomorrow she could not take our glory from us as it will be all we will get at present.

. . . If successful in the effort both the Government and the people of the US will be somewhat astonished. It is a noble scheme and will be highly noticed by our Government. If Mr. Read is not promoted to a Captaincy no man in the Navy deserves it. If nothing turns up against us this night will be an eventful [one] in the present war and also in the history of every man connected with it.

The sun slowly sank over Casco Bay, and against the dark protrusion of Cape Elizabeth the flash of Portland Head Light grew more distinct. The two fishermen were taken below, having in their ignorance of the true nature of the circumstances provided all the information Read required, including advice on the best channel for entry into the harbor. In shock and surprise, they discovered a large number of rough tars checking and loading weapons and making fire bombs. As their hands were tied and they were told to keep quiet, Bibber and Titcomb understood too late that these were not fishermen on a "frolic" but rather sailors of the Confederate Navy embarked on a daring raid deep inside Union territory. It was unthinkable, but nevertheless a reality.

Up on deck, with just a few of his sailors dressed in disguise for lookouts in the forts to see as the schooner passed near, Read watched for the channel markers and the prominent landmarks on the chart he had committed to memory. Local fishermen knew the way into Portland in fog and storm. They did not need charts. Being seen with one in hand as he guided the schooner in might spark suspicion. *Archer* rounded Cushing Island and headed north. She tacked against the offshore breeze that had come in late in the afternoon and rode the last of the incoming tide before slack water began and the ebb soon followed. Fort Preble perched on the hills to port, looking deadly, but Read did not fear the men inside it, nor did he intend to give them any cause to fire on his little ship. He had hatched a scheme expanded from the original inspiration that came when the fishermen told him about the cutter and steamer lying in Portland, and it depended on deception and surprise for success.

As the day passed, and the schooner made way swiftly across outer Casco Bay, Read had turned over in his mind the tantalizing opportunities for destruction. He broadened the goals of the mission to include firing the two gunboats under construction in the harbor, and perhaps, if he was lucky, the city as well. It would make a grand sight, the buildings ablaze, the citizens thrown into a confused panic, as if Robert E. Lee himself had suddenly sprung up in their midst. Leaving the city and shipping on fire astern he would continue to light the night sky with the glow of burning Yankee ships.

The closer Read got to Portland, the more excited he became about the raid. It was the ultimate realization of a dream that flared after the defeat aboard *McRea* on the lower Mississippi River, his beloved captain sprawled mortally wounded in a pool of blood on the warship's deck as the guns of the Union fleet pounded the small defending flotilla to pieces during the battle of New Orleans. He never forgot that day of invasion, of death and destruction in his homeland, and it was fitting somehow that his destiny had brought him to this potentially glorious moment of revenge.

Read's men shared similar emotions. They had come far from their ragtag, disharmonious condition at the outset of the voyage. They were now a dedicated fighting force willing to follow Read headlong into battle to fulfill their duty to the Confederacy. They were more dangerous than ever before.

The Portland Raid

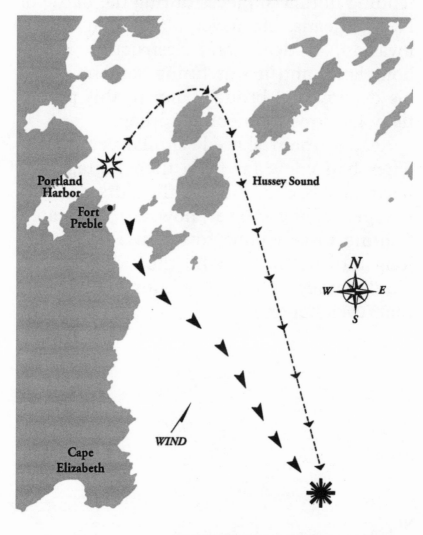

Portland
Harbor

Fort
Preble

Hussey Sound

N
W *E*
S

WIND

Cape
Elizabeth

✳	*Caleb Cushing* Captured
⇢--	*Caleb Cushing* Escapes
►	Union Pursuers
✸	Raiders Blow Up *Caleb Cushing*

Source: Official War Records

Chapter Eighteen

Surprise Attack

Portland Harbor, Dusk, June 26, 1863

The sun lingered long over Cape Elizabeth, casting shadows across the channel to darken the shores of the islands that served as a natural barrier to the fury of the storms that often screamed in off the Gulf of Maine. The last of the incoming tide flowed north past the city of Portland, too weak to overpower the force of the light offshore breeze and turn the vessels anchored in front of the piers stern to the wind. They rode bow to the inner reaches of Casco Bay, their bowsprits and jibbooms pointed toward the pleasant vista comprised of large and small islands dotting the immediate horizon. Ashore, the shops went dark as the keepers closed their businesses and hurried home to eat their Friday night suppers, the week's work done. Many of them looked forward to the party planned later that evening at the Ottawa House on Cushing Island, a favorite gathering place for revelry.

In the newspaper offices of the *Eastern Argus*, reporters finished their stories for the Saturday morning edition. Columns of type focused on the Confederate invasion. Special barbs were reserved for the Lincoln administration and for Fighting Joe Hooker, who appeared reluctant to fight. In fact, the writer need not have concerned himself with Hooker. The next day, at 1:00 p.m., when all of Portland's attention was riveted on a battle within earshot of the city, Fighting Joe telegraphed Washington asking to be relieved from duty for numerous reasons. His request was granted, and General George G. Meade, a native of Pennsylvania, took command of the army and prepared to fight Lee on an as yet undetermined battlefield. On the evening of June 26, the *Argus*'s editors wrote:

Gen. Lee keeps his plans to himself and Gen. Hooker seems disposed to allow him to carry them out without let or hindrance, to a certain point at least. At any rate no obstacle has been interposed as yet. We have never doubted that this aggressive campaign for which

Lee has been preparing for weeks, meant something that our people would not like, and that it should have been nipped in the bud. It was not, and every day it apparently grows more formidable! Such a force of veterans as he has now massed will make terrific work, whenever he chooses to strike the blow.

We should like to feel assured that Gen. Hooker or somebody else is prepared for him, but we do not. We, however, try to hope for the best, though fearing the worst. The incapacity at Washington is disgraceful, and the position, to us, unspeakably humiliating. With not less than 250,000 men altogether to checkmate Lee, he seems to go on in his operations without effective opposition, and to treat our forces with utter contempt.

As the senior editorial staff prepared the front pages, the junior writers completed the small notices tucked in the back of the newspaper. One of them involved a few sentences saying that Captain George Clarke, fifty-eight, had died the previous afternoon of dropsy and heart disease. The captain's death made news because he was the master of the revenue cutter *Caleb*

Cushing, at that very moment anchored off the Portland waterfront, half her men on liberty, with the balance of them aboard under the command of Lieutenant Dudley Davenport, a Georgian who had remained loyal to the Union after the war broke out and continued to serve in the Revenue Service. She was provisioned and loaded with ammunition for a two-month cruise. Clarke's replacement was on his way to take her to sea in search of *Tacony*. Adding his own opinion to the facts, the writer closed his paragraph about the cutter: "[The *Caleb Cushing*] will sail in search of the privateer Tacony as soon as [the new officer] comes, but unless the rebels are bold past belief they will be off before the Cushing can get on her track."

At the ferry landing, where the little steamboat pursued her runs to the inhabited islands of the bay, bringing provisions, mail, and passengers to and from Portland, the first wave of partyers gathered for the ride to Cushing Island. It was a beautiful, moonlit evening. The warm season had been late in coming to northern New England, as it often was. When the people in Washington suffered from the heat, tossing and turning unable to sleep, the citizens of Portland frequently snuggled under wool blankets, the windows of their homes closed tight against the cold of springtime. On this night, though, one of the first of the balmy summer, the well-dressed men on the dock wore only light jackets and the women wore shawls draped over their shoulders.

The partygoers gazed out at the harbor bathed in the soft, white light of the moon. The diminishing breeze was fragrant with the smell of wood smoke and pine. The boatmen called for them to board, and the ferry soon steamed away from the wharf, hooting her whistle as she went. She passed the gunboats at Franklin Wharf, the piles of freight on other nearby docks, and the New York steamer *Chesapeake* at her berth. She passed *Caleb Cushing*, with two watchmen in the stern, and several fishing smacks, all dark, their crews evidently ashore at the taverns or home with their wives and children. The steamboat made many trips, and as the night progressed her decks were more crowded on the return passage to Portland. The moon slowly crept downward in the sky. The wind dropped off until scarcely a ripple disturbed the smooth, black surface of the water. The tide ran out of the harbor, exposing rockweed on the ledges and mud on the clam flats.

The men of *Archer* waited with mounting anxiety, wondering what their captain intended to do in light of the developments of the evening. The unexpected forays of the steamboat filled with citizens of Portland, their raucous voices carrying across the water, as well as the bright moonlight demanded delay, if the raid was to hold any chance for success. Read stood on the aft deck of the schooner in the eclipse of shadow. The turn of events boded ill for him and his men. He had already given up hope of seizing the New York steamer based on the advice of engineer Brown during a conversation just after sunset, when the wind blew fair and the ebb tide appeared to favor them. But there were still options and he was ready to put them into action at the right time. All he needed was patience, a virtue he had been hard pressed to cultivate in his twenty-three years of life. Patience and a continuation of his good luck . . .

My engineer, Mr. Brown, expressed his doubts as to his ability to start the engines of the steamer proposed to be captured without the assistance of another engineer. I felt confident that Mr. Brown would do his utmost to perform the duty required of him, but as the nights were very short it was evident that if we failed to get the steamer underway, after waiting to get up steam, we could not get clear of the forts before we were discovered. As the wind was blowing moderately out of the harbor, I then decided to capture the cutter, and after getting from under the forts to return and fire the shipping.

Given the late hour, the lack of wind, and a tide soon to turn foul, the prospects of getting the cutter out of range of the forts in time to return in small boats to burn the shipping appeared bleak at best. Yet, as the moon set after midnight and Read observed deckhands securing the ferry in her berth, he mustered his crew on *Archer*'s deck for a surprise attack on *Caleb Cushing*. Leaving three men aboard the schooner, as well as Bibber and Titcomb, Read and his heavily armed sailors climbed quietly into two boats. They wrapped the oars and thole pins in rags to muffle the sounds of a rowboat under way, and in near silence, careful not to miss a stroke and cause a splash, the oarsmen rowed across the anchorage toward the cutter. How many Union sailors might confront them remained an open question, one that no doubt crossed the minds of all the raiders as they drew closer to their target.

Caleb Cushing loomed large in the semidarkness, backlit with a spread of stars so magnificent the scene might have captivated a casual observer. She was over one hundred feet in length, with a sharp, clipper bow. Her topsail schooner rig was tall and meant for speed on all points of sail, especially while beating to windward in chase of less fleet square-rigged vessels. On her quarter deck was a powerful thirty-two-pound pivot gun capable of inflicting lethal damage to flesh and bone, as well as to the wooden timbers of a ship. Its form and those of the watchmen standing near it were clearly visible. The boats closed with the cutter. The sentinels stirred, turned in the rebels' direction, and seeing them they cried, "Boats ahoy! Sheer off!"

The rebels rowed hard, disregarding stealth in favor of swift attack.

"Stand clear, there!"

The rebels rowed faster.

The men in the approaching boats did not appear to be harmless drunks come out from the taverns, which was the first logical conclusion. They now seemed to represent something more sinister, though the watchmen did not know exactly what. The guards ran below to raise the alarm, as their duty required.

The rebels reached the cutter and separated at the stern, ranging along each side of the vessel. In less than a minute, Read and his men swarmed up her sides, pistols and cutlasses in hand. They caught the guards as they came back up the companionway stairs, threatened to shoot them if they spoke, and clapped them in irons on deck. The raiders broke into two parties, one surging to the forecastle, the other aft to capture the officers. Four sailors reached the captain's cabin just as Lieutenant Davenport emerged rubbing his eyes with sleep. He stared in shock at the men, each of whom aimed a pistol at his head.

"Keep quiet or I'll blow your head off," one of the sailors said. "You are a prisoner of the Confederate States of America!"

Davenport complied.

Up forward, still at an advantage from the element of surprise, the rebels caught the nineteen crewmen as they were stirring awake or remained asleep in their hammocks. The Union men could not effectively resist the assault. However, one of them escaped through the forehatch intent on jumping overboard to alert the Army command stationed at Fort Preble. He dashed across the deck and was about to leap over the bulwark when several sailors grabbed him, "handling him roughly," according to the *Argus*, and soon subdued the would-be escapee. They took him below and shackled him in irons, holding him at gunpoint with the rest of his mates. Every Yankee aboard was threatened with "peril of their lives" if any made noise or tried further attempts to escape. *Caleb Cushing* was Read's in less than ten minutes.

It was now after one o'clock in the morning. The first hints of dawn would stain the eastern horizon over the Gulf of Maine a deep blue in less than four hours. Time ran short and Read knew it. Coordinating the efforts of his men, he dispatched a boat to *Archer* to pick up one of the fishermen, Albert Bibber, to serve as pilot while others prepared to let go the anchor chain. Still others scurried aloft and cast loose the gaskets securing the square sails in place, then returned to the deck to heave all the canvas up — the expansive main and foresail, as well as the main and foretopsail. The sails failed to ripple and thunder with life as they did in a good wind. They hung limp from the spars. The tide turned and the flood began, sending the ocean northward once again into the heart of Casco Bay and further hindering the rebel escape with the cutter.

A man rushed aft to consult with Read. Read listened and tried to mask his growing concern. The anchor chain could not be easily let go, making for a speedy departure under tow from the two boats stationed forward, the strongest of his crew at the oars. "Very well. Heave the anchor up," Read said, "and look lively."

The clatter from the anchor chain rattling through the hawshole sounded frightfully loud in the quiet of the early morning. It attracted the notice of a man ashore, who stopped, wondered why the cutter was getting under way, and went home without thinking much more about the strange sight in the harbor. The rebel sailors resisted the urge to curse and grunt as they worked the capstan, pushing against the bars to turn the drum. They broke into a heavy sweat, in part from their exertions, but also from the fear that began to descend upon them. They all knew the precarious nature of their situation, and that knowledge imbued them with the vigor of desperation. A half hour passed, and the men finally hauled the anchor up.

Caught in an eddy of the incoming tide, strengthening by the moment, the cutter spun round and suddenly came to a gentle stop, her keel lodged in the soft mud of the harbor.

Read showed no emotion. According to Bibber, who was on deck with him, he stayed calm. He directed the men in one of the boats to row a line over to a nearby ship. Once the warp was secured, the rebels aboard the cutter manned the capstan again, this time to put tension on the line to stretch it bar tight.

"Belay haul," Read whispered, and the order was relayed to the men forward.

The rebels waited. It was now nearing 2:30 a.m. Dawn would soon arrive, and danger with it. The tide continued to rise. The cutter stirred. The motion was hardly perceptible. Yet, in a short time she was free as her bow swung round to face the sea, riding to the current with no wind to influence her position tethered like a tender to the neighboring ship.

"Capstan haul," Read said.

The men worked the capstan, their chests to the bars, circling the drum. The light steps of their feet beat a rhythm on the dew-moistened deck. The cutter drew closer to her neighbor, vacant and quiet, the crew ashore. Satisfied he was in deep water, Read ordered the tow boats at the bow to get under way. The oarsmen bent to their work with a will. The towlines went taut.

"Cast off warp," Read said.

The line secured to the adjacent vessel splashed into the water. *Caleb Cushing* floated free. The two rowboats on station off the bow, each with a line led to the bitts, seemed to stand still even as the crews rowed as hard as they could. However, those aboard the cutter noted her moving forward and how the current set her to the north as she came across the main channel close to the fort on Gorges Island, a mere black projection against the sky. The fort was evidently unmanned, a bit of good fortune for the raiders. She made way slowly eastward along the land side of Little Diamond Island, with Great Diamond visible as a dark expanse off the starboard bow. *Archer* remained at anchor, awaiting enough of a breeze to get underway to follow and rendezvous offshore, where the prisoners would be transferred to her and set free once clear of the coast and any pursuers that might take up a chase.

Due to Read's study of the charts, he was

well aware that a series of ledges lay to starboard. They surrounded Fort Gorges and extended north as well. There were also shoal areas of mud to contend with. He dared not cut too close to the hazards. Inexplicably, he did not ask Bibber for advice. He calculated his drift from the incoming tide and concluded that the current would push him clear, and he was correct. *Caleb Cushing* skirted the rocks and mud banks and continued her progress east toward Hussey Sound, an alternate to the main channel into Portland, and a waterway devoid of any fortifications.

The cutter drew abreast of Great Diamond Island. Hussey Sound lay dead off the starboard beam on the other side of the land blocking them from the open sea. Slowly and steadily, the rebels towed their prize onward. Read felt the first puff of a southerly breeze on the back of his neck, which was damp with sweat. He glanced aloft and saw the sails start to luff. Tiny ripples formed on the water, their presence made known from the lapping against the hull. The darkness to starboard lessened, and a passage hove into view between the tip of Great Diamond and much smaller Cow Island. The sails filled and the cutter came alive, gathering way at last from her broad expanse of canvas.

Read turned to Bibber. "Can we get through that channel?"

"That's a very bad passage," Bibber replied. "The cutter is deep and the water shallow."

Caleb Cushing picked up speed. Read ordered the men at the oars aboard and the boats secured astern for towing.

"Take her in," he said to the helmsman.

The opening between the two islands was narrow, and though the tide was on the flood it had not yet covered the tops of the ledges submerged at high water. They rose up on either side of the cutter. The breeze increased. The sailors trimmed the sheets. She sped into the gap and toward the clear water of Hussey Sound beyond. The shores seemed to close in and all went dark, the ambient light lost save for off the bow, like a beacon to guide her through. Far to the east, the first light of dawn illuminated the Gulf of Maine.

Caleb Cushing sailed clear of Cow Island and passed the mouth of Diamond Cove. She cut close to Crow Island, more a nub of rock than anything, and surged into Hussey Sound with a fair wind funneled through Diamond Pass, a passage between Great Diamond and Peaks Island. Once in the lee of Peaks, the cutter slowed, her wind temporarily blocked. The features of the land were visible in the predawn light, and they became more easily discerned.

In the harbors and coves, the lobstermen and coastal fishers readied their boats for the day's work. Some were already at sea, hauling trawls in the waters above offshore ledges and reefs. On the farms around Portland, the men milked cows and prepared for their labors in the fields. In the city, while many of the residents slept soundly after the night's festivities, stevedores and longshoremen awoke to start work loading the rest of the freight aboard the New York steamer *Chesapeake*.

Caleb Cushing soon left Peaks Island astern. Clear of the close proximity to land, the light breeze strengthened. She left a small wake, and the rowboats kicked up tiny bow waves. Portland Head Light flashed off the starboard beam. Suddenly, the lights of a steamer bound for the main channel into Portland appeared. She was the Boston transport *Forest City*, ahead of schedule. Aboard her was the replacement for the deceased Captain Clarke, the officer charged with taking *Caleb Cushing* to sea to hunt down the rebel pirates on the infamous bark *Tacony*. The vessels passed each other and the distance between them widened. The steamer held her course for Portland Harbor and the cutter steered for the open ocean.

Forest City passed another much smaller craft, a schooner under full sail, the fishing smack *Archer*. *Forest City* steamed past Fort Preble and rounded up in readiness to come to her berth. When all lines were secured, the steamer safe at the pier, her crew went below to their bunks to rest. The passengers stirred awake, hungry for their breakfasts. One of them, Lieutenant James H. Merryman, United States Revenue Service, was up early. He dressed and went out on deck to admire his new command. He glanced around at the vessels anchored in the harbor. Odd, he thought. Very odd indeed. Where on earth was *Caleb Cushing*?

Merryman was not the only one to find the missing cutter a puzzle that needed solving, and solving fast. Up in the marine observation tower on Munjoy Hill, the lookout spied the cutter making her way out to sea under full sail in a light breeze. She passed through a fleet of fishing boats working the waters around Cod Ledge, about three miles off the tip of Cape Elizabeth. He had received no indication the cutter was supposed to leave the harbor on this day.

Down on the waterfront, the half of *Caleb Cushing*'s crew on liberty returned to resume their duties. Finding their ship gone without orders, and meeting their new captain, they immediately raised the alarm. The first person they sent for was Jedediah Jewett, Collector of Customs for the port of Portland, the man answering directly to Secretary of the Treasury Salmon P. Chase. At approximately ten minutes after eight, several men rushed to Jewett's home and pounded on the door. Perplexed at the commotion, he answered the door and was greeted with a flurry of reports. The cutter was gone. The Southern-born Lieutenant Davenport and his traitorous cohorts had stolen her! They had gone to join the pirate *Tacony*!

The news obviously alarmed Jewett. *Caleb Cushing* was armed with a 32-pounder pivot and a 12-pound Dahlgren gun forward. She carried about 400 pounds of powder and ninety rounds for the pivot gun, along with ammunition for the smaller cannon. In the hands of traitors, the harm she might do to U.S. merchantmen was potentially enormous. *Tacony* had proven that all too well in recent days. Jewett took immediate and decisive action. In his report to Secretary Chase, he described the coordinated efforts of the soldiers and citizens of Portland acting under his orders:

I was advised at my house at ten minutes past 8 a.m. that the cutter had gone to sea, and regret that my suspicions, as I now think unjustly, fell upon First Lieutenant Davenport as the party who had run off with her.

I at once came to the conclusion that this was an exigency when I ought not to wait for orders from you, but assume the responsibility of her recapture for the Government. I at once sent messengers to Fort Preble for guns and men of the Seventeenth Regulars, to be ready for a steamer that I would have at the port wharf; also sent a messenger to Camp Lincoln, to Colonel Mason, of the Seventh Maine Volunteers, for men.

To both these requests the responses were promptly made, and in less than one hour Colonel Mason had all the men at camp, including his band, in the city and on board of the steamers. I at once chartered the *Forest City*, a 700-ton side-wheel steamer of the Boston

Line, and also the small steamer *Casco* as a transport to take the guns and men from Fort Preble wharf; the steamer *Forest City* drawing too much water to lie at it. I also chartered a steam-tug propeller and sent her to the upper bridge in our harbor to take on board the men of the Seventh, and as evidence of the prompt response to my calls I would state that in fifty minutes after I had learned of the capture of the cutter three steamers had left the wharf to overhaul her. [Actually, it took almost two hours]

Finding that at the suggestion of the mayor the steamer *Chesapeake* (propeller), of the New York Line, was getting up steam, I put Colonel Mason and the largest portion of his command on board of her, she having obtained two brass 6-pounders from the State arsenal. She also had about 50 citizen volunteers of all ages and colors, who armed themselves and repaired on board.

By nine o'clock, crowds of men, women, and children filled the city of Portland. The anger among the citizens at the supposed traitor Davenport and those with him verged on a mob frenzy. It was simply too much for them to stand that a traitor had lain hidden in their midst, swapping stories and lifting pints with the Mainers at the taverns, and proudly wearing the uniform of a Revenue Service officer. Men ran to their homes, snatched up their muskets or rifles, and rushed to the waterfront. Every man who could find a place on board the passenger steamers pushed his way up the gangplank. *Forest City* set off first. Three steam tugs also got underway, and *Chesapeake* departed a short time later. Just before she sailed, her captain asked the mayor of Portland, Captain Jacob McLellan, for any further instructions other than to overhaul and retake the cutter.

"Catch the damned scoundrels and hang every one of them," McLellan said.

The crowd cheered.

Chesapeake got underway and headed down the main channel at flank speed.

Chapter Nineteen

FINAL BATTLE

*At Sea, 15 Miles Off Portland Head Light,
10:30 a.m., June 27, 1863*

A slight haze obscured Cape Elizabeth,
fading the bold features of the land into a
dark smudge atop the gray-blue swells as
Caleb Cushing glided south-southeast on the
heels of the gentle morning breeze. More
than a dozen small craft lay astern. The
crews busy fishing over Cod Ledge remained
oblivious to the danger that had passed so
near, though not for long. They, too, appeared to recede into the white glare from
the sun's reflection on the water and the
wisps of light mist shrouding the Gulf of
Maine. Read stood on the quarter deck of
the cutter and peered through his spyglass to
the northwest past the headland marking the
outer approaches to Portland Harbor. Two
plumes of black smoke caught his eye, and

he squinted to get a better look.

The men on deck followed their captain's gaze. The hulls of the ships beneath the smoke became visible as time passed. Two steamers. Both on intercept courses. All was silent save for the sound of the sea washing against the cutter's bow and along the sides of the hull aft to the transom, the tap of halyards against the masts, and the occasional groan from the vessel's timbers. To a man, the fatigue of the previous weeks slowed their efforts, as if it became a weight carried over many miles on a rough and dangerous road. Each sailor anxiously watched as the steamers sped toward the cutter, still miles away, but closing fast. They thought of the duty that now called once again, though this time with death as the potential price for its execution.

Read lowered his glass and turned to his first officer. "We will beat to quarters, Mr. Brown," he said.

"Aye, sir," Brown responded, and shouted orders to the crew.

The steamer *Forest City* sped through the swells, her paddle wheels beating the water and churning up a prodigious wake. Eager to fight, her company of soldiers and citizens clasped their muskets and rifles. On the forecastle deck were two small field guns taken from Fort Preble. They were no match for the heavy cannon aboard the cutter, but the gunners prepared for combat hoping for a lucky shot that might bring down the masts of the chase and enable them to board with overwhelming force. Two boats were towed astern to serve as troop transports. As the steamer powered onward, a wave caught the boats, immediately swamping them. The painters snapped and the boats disappeared.

Forest City drew within range of *Caleb Cushing*, and the rebels opened fire. The report from the cannon carried across the water all the way to Munjoy Hill in Portland, where a crowd searched the distant horizon with spyglasses, but could see little through the haze. However, a reporter for the *Eastern Argus* was aboard the steamer *Chesapeake*. He described the moment of engagement as he observed it, jotting the events down in his notebook as quickly as possible.

[Caleb Cushing] rounds to, a flash is seen, and the sound of the first gun comes booming over the water. "That means business," says Captain Leighton, [Naval Inspector] who with

Colonel Mason and others were watching her from the top of the pilot house. "Hurra," says a private of the 7th Maine who had evidently listened to the music before. "Steer for her," says Captain Leighton to the pilot, "and we'll run her down or go to the bottom." It was now evident that there was to be some lively work.

Her pivot gun blazing, sending several shots toward her pursuers in rapid succession, *Caleb Cushing* tacked and sailed straight toward *Forest City* in a head-on maneuver that surprised the experienced military men from Maine. They did not expect the hunted to turn in a bold and brash attempt to inflict the most damage possible, like a cornered wild animal desperate to escape. With her superior guns, the cutter closing fast posed a serious danger. Read's men fired again, and a column of white water erupted thirty feet from the intended target. The steamer retreated and awaited the arrival of *Chesapeake*, a faster vessel, with the added advantage of having bales of cotton stacked on her decks to act as barriers against solid shot and minie balls.

Read's move may have surprised the

Army officers, but it terrified the citizen volunteers. Unlike some of the veterans among the soldiers, they had never witnessed battle. For them, war smacked of romance and glory. The sudden realization that someone might die dampened their enthusiasm for the chase, and many wanted to turn back, wishing they had stayed in Portland.

"The steamer was filled with citizens without any knowledge of the responsibilities of the situation, and who apparently had left the harbor for a pleasure trip," wrote Captain Nathaniel Prime, 17th Infantry, U.S. Army, in his report on the engagement. "The accumulated advice and disjointed comments of these bewildered the captain, who stopped his boat and awaited the arrival of the propeller *Chesapeake*. . . ."

Forest City lay hove to, still within range of the cutter, as *Chesapeake* came on under a full head of steam. She cut through the waves, lifting her bow to each with a flash of white foam. The luck of the Union men held. No shots had hit yet, though Read's men were finding the range and bearing. The accuracy of the gunnery improved, and it seemed inevitable that bloodshed loomed near at hand.

"Another gun from the cutter, as we kept

on, and this time the shot is intended for us. It is a ricochet shot, and the ball comes skipping along the water directly towards us, but falls short, and the men indulge in a laugh; at the same time they admit that the shot is a good one," the *Argus* reporter wrote.

Chesapeake fired back with her small cannon, missing the cutter.

The two steamers converged, ranged close, and stopped side by side, while the respective commanders aboard shouted back and forth as they worked out the best plan of attack. After a few moments, *Chesapeake* proceeded on her way, taking the lead in the assault. "We shall steer straight for her and run into her any way we can, and you can take what's left!" Captain Leighton said to his counterpart on board *Forest City*. The main objective now was to hit the cutter amidships and rake her deck with rifle fire to kill any rebels caught in the open. After the initial volley, the soldiers were to board and dispatch the rest with bayonets.

Both crews cheered. "Huzzah! Huzzah! Huzzah!" they cried. "Stand by the flag!"

Chesapeake closed in on the rebels. The deck of the cutter appeared crowded with men, some of whom were boarding a longboat. The tension and excitement of the soldiers and citizens of the steamer increased. The reporter from the *Argus* wrote furiously in his notebook.

It is the opinion that her intention is to board us, and preparations are accordingly made to "welcome them with bloody hands to hospitable graves." The voice of Colonel Mason is heard, and "stand ready, men" is the watchword. The boat nears us — she is filled — bang and the grape come whistling forward, aft and over us, but no one is hit, — the smoke clears up. . . .

Chesapeake returned fire, and under orders from Captain Leighton the pilot spun the wheel, turning to ram the longboat just off the bow. The men stopped rowing and waved white handkerchiefs in the air, shouting for them to sheer off. Just before the collision, the pilot steered clear. The boat banged against the hull, which smashed bits of wood from the gunwales, almost swamping as the ship continued forward through the water, riding on from her own momentum. The pilot rang to the engineers below for full astern. The propeller backed. Foam tumbled and boiled, and eddies whirled the sea.

"We are the cutter's crew! For God's sake, don't fire!" Lieutenant Davenport screamed, staring up the clifflike sides of the ship in shock and dismay at the dozens of guns pointing down at him and his men.

The citizens aimed their weapons, shouting, "Shoot 'em! Kill 'em! Hang 'em!"

Captain Leighton drew his pistol and aimed it at a crowd of men near the bulwark, his face stern, his jaw set in anger and determination. The pistol cocked and ready, he said, "Hold! The first man that fires shall be shot; I am not a pirate to fire on a flag of truce."

The men in the boat scrambled up a Jacob's ladder. Some found the task difficult because of the irons still shackled to their wrists. Lieutenant Davenport was among the first to board the steamer. In a "violently agitated" state, according to the *Argus*, he said, "It is hard, after a man has been taken prisoner, ironed, and his life threatened by pirates, to be shot by his own friends!"

The people of *Chesapeake* and *Forest City*, as well as the steam tugs circling nearby, owed Davenport much, possibly their lives. The so-called grape that whistled over them and through the rigging consisted of iron nails and spikes, bits of chain, even stone. It was not conventional grapeshot, and it represented the last desperate attempt of the rebels to stave off the inevitable end of their voyage. Read and his men were unable to find the ninety rounds of shot for the 32-pound pivot gun hidden behind a mirror in a special locker located in the captain's cabin. The rest of the ammunition was stowed behind the powder bags out of view and also went undiscovered. After a complete search of the cutter, Read's men found less than a dozen rounds, and thus resorted to firing anything they could scavenge at the approaching steamers. Davenport had told Read nothing, though Read repeatedly questioned him, even saying during his various conversations with Davenport, "As a Southern born man, you ought to be ashamed of yourself."

As Davenport and his men were taken below for questioning, the attention of the ship's company turned back to *Caleb Cushing*. White smoke poured from the main hatch and through the open companionway aft. Two boats full of men put off from the cutter and began rowing hard for shore. Unwilling to give up, Read and his sailors were determined to make an escape, even as it appeared impossible. The steamer *Forest City* bore down on them, under orders from Lieutenant J. H. Merryman. Neither Merryman nor anyone else on his steamer knew that these were the very men more than thirty U.S. Navy ships had been searching for since June 13. The identity of the rebels soon became clear, however. Merryman wrote in his report to Secretary of the Treasury Salmon P. Chase:

. . . Two more boats left the [*Caleb Cushing*], and instantly smoke and flames were seen bursting from her wardroom and cabin companionways. By the aid of my glasses I perceived that her decks were deserted and that the *Cushing* was doomed to destruction. Expecting every moment to see her blown to atoms, for I had learned that her magazine contained 500 pounds of powder, I advised Captain Liscomb to bear away for the boats containing the pirates and run them down. As we neared them, however, they frantically displayed white handkerchiefs and Masonic signs, and the steamer was therefore sheered clear of them and stopped.

Merryman rushed to the bulwark as the boats came alongside. A small man with a brown mustache and goatee was the first to climb the Jacob's ladder and come aboard. He looked haggard, his face grim and strained. He stood erect and at attention in full possession of his dignity as he withdrew his two pistols from under his blue frock coat and presented them butt first to Merryman.

"I am Second Lieutenant Charles W. Read, Confederate States Navy, late of the CSS *Florida*. Your prisoner, sir."

Merryman accepted the guns and took Read aside to question him while the rest of the rebels were tied up and put below. As the men talked, *Caleb Cushing* burned. The flames eventually reached the sails and the standing rigging. For Read, the burning ship was a familiar sight. For the Union men, it was not. The onlookers stared at the inferno, transfixed at the scene. A half-hearted, abortive attempt was made to save the cutter, but the ill-advised endeavor resulted in nothing more than the salvage of a small boat at the peril of those involved. At approximately 2:00 p.m., the fire reached the magazine. The explosion that followed was observed and heard on Munjoy Hill more than fifteen miles away. Closer to the action, the *Argus* reporter wrote in his typical breathless prose. . . .

. . . A terrific explosion shakes the very heavens. The smoke rolls up in vast columns, fragments of shells, masts and spars and blackened timbers are seen hundreds of feet in the air, falling all around, the cutter begins to sink, her stem disappears, the guns fall off the deck into the fathomless deep, she careens, she gives one lurch — and the *Caleb Cushing* sinks beneath the waves. The only remaining mast disappears, but soon rises some fifteen or twenty feet above the water, then sinks to rise no more.

Dozens of small craft converged on the wreckage and picked debris from the water. A small boat came alongside *Forest City*. Albert Bibber, whom Read released just prior to the start of the engagement, hailed the officers. He was quickly taken aboard and told the commanders about the schooner *Archer*, still at large and sailing eastward past Jewel Island. Bibber pointed at the schooner visible on the horizon. "There she is! She's got more rebels aboard her, men!"

Forest City put about and under full steam shortly overhauled *Archer*, firing a shot across her bow. The rebels brazenly sailed on.

The gunners trained the cannons on the schooner, ready to fire. Her small crew rounded to. The sails luffed. *Archer* slowed and began to make way to leeward. A boat was put over the side of the steamer, and three Confederate sailors were taken aboard, as well as Titcomb. Deckhands secured a towline to the schooner, and *Forest City* headed for Whitehead Passage, then on to Portland Harbor, cruising in company with *Chesapeake* until they separated, the latter vessel favoring the main channel past Cushing Island.

As the ships came in, the men aboard shouted and cheered. The shoreline was full of people, all shouting with joy and excitement. The cannons at Fort Preble roared in salute to the victors, sending clouds of gray smoke drifting down the hills toward the water. The two steamers fired in response, and many of the citizen volunteers pointed their muskets skyward and pulled the trigger. It sounded as if a new battle had begun.

As we passed the forts in the harbor

guns were fired, bells rang and other lively demonstrations were made. The wharves and all available points were alive with people, who cheered again and again, and they were responded to from the decks of the *Chesapeake* by cheers and the firing of guns.

Once ashore, the prisoners were put under a double guard, bayonets fixed and pointed at the throng that pressed in on all sides. The crowd went crazy with bloodlust. Screams of "Hang them! Hang the pirates!" filled the air. The troops surrounded the prisoners to protect them from the furious mob and hustled down Commercial Street, anxious to reach Fort Preble as quickly as possible. Upon arriving, they escorted the Confederates to cells. As night fell, people remained crowded outside the fort talking of the day's battle and the capture of the rebel pirates who had boldly raided the city.

Outrage at the audacity of the rebels boiled among the politicians. Most upset was Mayor McLellan, who regarded the raid on Portland as a personal affront, and the rebels as mere criminals. While the crowd was still gathered outside of Fort Preble, a band of police arrived. Under orders from McLellan, they had come to take the pirates to jail, and most wished to hang them from the nearest tree. The chief of police demanded that the commander, Major George L. Andrews, turn over the captives.

In some respects, the mayor and the police were correct in their assertion that Read and his men were pirates and should be treated as such. Read had skated close to piracy as he rampaged up the coast, and certainly to the merchants and fishermen he was a "desperado" or "freebooter." But he did not cross the line. His actions were taken as an officer of the Confederate Navy and he adhered to most, if not all, of the rules governing commerce destroyers. Further, Read had wisely surrendered to Merryman, a marine in the Revenue Service, who then turned him and his men over to the U.S. Army as prisoners of war. Andrews explained this to the police, and refused to release the prisoners to the local authorities. The police departed, expressing their disappointment, though Andrews had reassured them that the rebels were well guarded and could not possibly escape. The crowd dispersed as well. With the excitement and antagonism in Portland running high, Andrews wrote the following to Assistant Adjutant General Major C. T.

Christensen, Department of the East, New York City:

> You can form but a faint idea of the excitement now existing among the citizens of Portland and vicinity. Rumor follows rumor [about additional raids] in rapid succession. . . . I would respectfully suggest that the prisoners be sent from here as quietly and expeditiously as possible, as I do not think it safe for them to be placed in the custody of the citizens, and, while the present excitement continues, I feel obliged to mount so large a guard that one-half of my force are on duty every night.

Word spread fast about the presence of Confederates in the cells of Fort Preble, and stories of what they had done as they cruised up the coast became more colorful with each telling. Outside of those in the military, most people had never seen a rebel before, and while Read and his men were considered dangerous they also became a major curiosity. Large crowds surrounded the fort the day following the battle, hoping for a look at them. The record is not clear as to how, but it appears that souvenir hunters made off with what little spare clothing Read and his men had. Read later wrote in a preliminary report to Mallory, secretary of the Confederate Navy, "As all of our clothing was distributed as relics to the people of Portland, I beg that you will, if possible, remit to Assistant Paymaster Nixon a sufficient sum of money to purchase my men a change of clothing."

The press insisted on seeing the prisoners. On the afternoon of June 28, a pack of newsmen, among them the reporter for the *Eastern Argus*, asked Major Andrews for permission to interview the rebels.

"Gentlemen, you may speak with the prisoners only with their permission to do so," he said.

Read agreed to talk with the reporters, seeing it as an opportunity to spread more fear among the Yankees. The tales of destruction would be published in the North's largest newspapers and remind citizens of the Union that the war could indeed come to them, just as it seemed to be in Pennsylvania at that very moment as Lee advanced. If raids occurred in Maine, so far from the front lines, a rebel raider might well appear anywhere at any time. It was a prospect bound to create anxiety, and that thought must have pleased Read. He could still do good for the Confederacy even if he was sitting in prison.

Read, his second in command, Brown, along with three other members of his crew, stood up as the journalists entered the cell. They shook hands all around, as if old friends, and Read began to relate the events that had transpired since May 6 when he first set off aboard *Clarence* to carry out his mission.

Lieut. Read, in giving us the full particulars of the cruise . . . was very quiet and gentlemanly in his demeanor. His answers were briefly given, being evidently well studied before he replied. Not a smile irradiated his thin, sharp face, and he was not disposed to communicate any more than he was asked. His reticence in this respect showed much shrewdness. Sometimes when a question was asked him, he maintained a profound silence, which was not broken when one of the others voluntarily replied in his stead.

Read was careful not to reveal too much, feeding the journalists just enough information to stir up the readers. He also sprinkled in a bit of disinformation. He planted the idea that there were other commerce destroyers nearby, and that CSS *Florida* was on her way to blow up every merchant vessel she met with in the waters of northern New England. These rumors were already circulating through cities and towns up and down the coast. And, to the officials, who had confiscated Read's papers and Drayton's diary, the threat of additional Confederate raiders appeared quite real indeed, given that it was clear from both Read and Drayton's writings that they had fully expected to meet *Florida* in the vicinity of Nantucket.

Evidently, the crew were also quite happy to share stories of their exploits. As the newsmen entered their cell across from Read's, they were singing songs of the Confederacy, apparently in fine spirits and as defiant as ever in spite of their captivity. "As the [crew] gave us the particulars, they smiled at intervals, especially when the oft repeated 'burnt her' was mentioned in regard to the long list of captures," the *Argus* reporter wrote.

The reporters left Read and his men satisfied that they had gotten their stories, and hurried off to file their copy. An agent for the Associated Press soon had his dispatch ready and telegraphed it to New

York. Dusk fell, with the usual cool of a late June evening in Maine. The people of Portland slept soundly, knowing that at least one Confederate raider would never take to the sea again, but there was uneasiness among the citizens and officials. Might not other Confederates lurk nearby?

At around 3:10 a.m. on the morning of June 29, church bells began ringing all over Portland. Men rode on horseback through the streets shouting, "A rebel gunboat is inside of Cape Lights and men are being landed!" As people opened their doors, rubbing sleep from their eyes, they joined their neighbors in front of their homes. Fear began to build, and husbands and fathers rushed inside to get their guns.

At 3:20 a.m., the *New York Times* received the following dispatch from Portland: "A general alarm has just aroused the whole city with wild rumor, that a gunboat is landing men below the Fort. It must of course be humbug, but two men have come over from Cape Elizabeth with the alarm."

Major Andrews mustered all of his troops, placing extra guards on Read and his men. Then the soldiers waited, guns with fixed bayonets pointed into the darkness. Soon, word came that there was no gunboat. No Confederates landing. It was all a hoax, but it was a very real indicator of the degree of fear Read had created in the minds of the common citizen residing on the coast of New England.

With a handful of men, a tiny howitzer, and nothing more than pistols and rifles, Read had captured and burned close to two dozen merchant vessels, causing millions in financial losses. His voyage was emblematic of the Confederacy's uncanny ability to inflict great damage on the Union with scant resources. Doing much with little appeared to be the case in most every aspect of the conflict, and in this Read succeeded grandly.

Read did not leave a trail of dead in his wake. Not one person died as a direct result of his actions. And he did not take joy in burning beautiful ships or in depriving hard-working fishermen of a means to make a living. He did his duty. That was all. It was simply the way of it in war.

AFTERMATH

CHARLES W. READ

Scarcely three weeks after arriving at Fort Warren in outer Boston Harbor, Read and three other Confederates he had met attempted to escape from prison. They collected a number of empty two-gallon bottles to serve as floats for a makeshift raft, some strips of canvas to use as lashings, and a length of rope to help them climb fifteen feet down a stone wall, after wiggling through a V-shaped slit built into their chamber to enable riflemen to fire on attackers. On a tempestuous night, August 16, 1863, the four men squeezed through the rifle slit and reached the shore undetected, where they assembled the raft and plunged into the sea. In less than an hour, struggling against the swift tide and suffering from hypothermia because of the cold water, the men were near drowning. They returned to the fort and crept back to their cells the same way they had left. The guards did not notice their brief absence.

Undaunted, the men recruited two additional members to join their escape group, both of whom were strong swimmers charged with the duty of swimming to an adjacent island to steal a boat. If successful, they would return for the rest and all of them would sail to Canada. On the night of August 18, the Confederates escaped a second time, reached the shore, and the two strongest swimmers set off, evidently drowning in their attempt to reach the island. Two others followed, and succeeded in commandeering a small sailboat, though too late to return for Read and the other man. The two sailed as far as New Hampshire before they were caught, and when they were sent back to Fort Warren they discovered Read and his friend had been detected on their way to the cell, and all four were placed in solitary confinement.

After the four escapees finally rejoined the general prison population, they noticed that bars had been added to the rifle slits in all the cells to prevent any additional escape attempts. The men were also kept under a close watch, but it did no good. Read found another route to freedom, this time through an old, defunct chimney. Working long into the night for months with a jackknife and an ice pick, he chipped away at the loose stone and brick to make an opening just wide enough to squeeze through. The last stages of the renovation required him to stand on the shoulders of a man below in order to reach the top of the chimney. His fellow prisoners helped hide the excavated fragments of brick and stone.

Though there is no exact date on record, it is known that Read and his friend from the two earlier forays escaped up the enlarged chimney during the winter of 1864. Once they were outside, the guards almost discovered them. They quickly hid under some canvas. One of the sentries stabbed the covering with his bayonet to see if there was anyone under it, driving the blade deep into Read's thigh. Despite the searing pain, he did not cry out. He overheard the sentry say that his bayonet was wet to the other guard, who warned him it might rust. He wiped the blade on the canvas and both men moved on. When they were gone, Read's friend helped him swim to a sailboat moored off the fort. The salt water soaked into the wound, adding to Read's agony. He almost bled to death.

They were gone for only a short time before a gunboat picked them up and brought them back to Fort Warren.

Read was returned to the Confederacy during a prisoner exchange in October 1864. Limping from his wound, the sight in his right eye partially and permanently impaired from the bits of limestone and powder that covered his face while he was digging out the chimney at Fort Warren, he was in constant physical pain. He had also lost a considerable amount of weight. With so little to spare in the first place, he looked distinctly skeletal, but his zeal to fight for his country had not diminished. If anything, it had increased.

In the coming months, Read served as an artillery officer on the James River, relishing the cannon duels with the Yanks on the opposite shore. He commanded torpedo boats engaged in an attempt to free the James River squadron for an attack on Union positions downriver. In addition, he concocted a daring scheme to cart torpedo boats overland behind Union lines, where he would relaunch them to blow up U.S. Navy ships that blockaded the river and kept the small Confederate fleet penned in. The mission failed, but Read brought his men safely back to Confederate lines, though many of them had nearly frozen to death during the expedition.

Read's last assignment took him back to the deep South in the winter of 1865 as master of one of the last Confederate rams left afloat, CSS *William H. Webb*. Again, he dreamed up a bold plan. It involved refitting the vessel on the Red River in Louisiana, then taking her to sea with a shipment of cotton to sell in Cuba to raise funds for the faltering Confederacy. By the time the work on the ram was completed and Read was ready to make a run to the Gulf of Mexico through a gauntlet of Union vessels, spring had come. Lee surrendered at Appomattox Court House on April 9, and, on April 15, President Lincoln died after the shooting the previous evening at Ford's Theater. Although Confederate forces were still engaged in the West, the war was essentially over.

Read set off with *Webb* on April 16, 1865 and slowly made his way down the Red River. Each passing day and mile brought him closer to its outlet into the Mississippi and the 300-mile dash to the Gulf of Mexico. While taking on wood in Alexandria, Read learned of Lee's surrender and Lincoln's assassination. Just as important, he also learned that the Union Navy was waiting for him on the Mississippi. Nevertheless, he resolved to proceed with the mission as long as there was hope for the Confederate forces to regain their footing and continue the fight.

On April 23, Read took the ram down the last of the Red River and into the Mississippi. For most of the next day, under fire at times, and with the U.S. Navy in pursuit, *Webb* steamed down the river toward the Gulf of Mexico, stopping now and then to allow her crew to cut the telegraph lines leading to Union ports downriver. The tactic worked. Read remained one step ahead of his hunters, just as he had in the cruise of *Clarence*, *Tacony*, and *Archer*. In fact, he used deception quite effectively. At one point, as *Webb* passed through New Orleans, he ordered his men to dress in Union uniforms they had obtained and to lounge on deck smoking their pipes, with the Union flag at half-mast in honor of Lincoln. Men aboard the Union Navy ships they passed called out asking if they had seen the rebel ram.

Webb steamed on. She was almost beyond the city limits when one of the Union ships opened fire. Read ordered the ram to full speed and sped downriver under heavy cannonading, the Confederate flag flying proudly. Approximately fifty miles above forts Jackson and St. Philip, *Webb* encountered a Union warship she could not escape. Read ran the ram aground, set her ablaze, and surrendered to the U.S. Navy. The man who formally accepted him as a prisoner of war was a former classmate from Annapolis.

Read was sent back to Fort Warren, arriving once again on May 10 at the place he loathed. The war was all but over. In fact, the last major rebel force still in the field surrendered on May 26, 1865. Read applied for permission to take the oath of allegiance and return to Mississippi, but his request was not acted upon immediately. Rebel officers graduated from West Point or Annapolis were temporarily denied the option of pledging their allegiance to the United States in return for release from prison. Time passed. On June 21, Read wrote an appeal to President Andrew Johnson asking that he might be allowed to take the oath of amnesty. He received no response. However, Read was soon thereafter granted amnesty, and allowed to take the oath of allegiance to the United States. He was released from Fort Warren on July 24. The most exciting period of his life was over.

Read lived the rest of his days in obscurity, finally settling in to a long stint as a Mississippi River pilot and as Harbor Master of New Orleans. He married Rozaltha G. Hall on December 3, 1867, nearly seven years after their first meeting. They had six children, three of whom lived to adulthood. Relatively speaking, the marriage was a happy one, their lives together comfortable. Unfortunately, it was also fairly short. Rozaltha died of yellow fever in 1878, leaving behind two young children and an infant for Read to care for. Read married again in 1884, and the couple had a child the following year. Again, the marriage was not to last for very long. In 1889, Read contracted a disease of the kidneys and his health declined. He died of pneumonia on January 25, 1890, at the age of forty-nine.

Read may have lived and died in relative obscurity, but he was not totally forgotten. In 1879, the Sons of Confederate Veterans awarded him the Medal of Honor. His deeds during the war were mentioned in his obituary. And a classmate of his from Annapolis, who was bound for great fame at the battle of Manila Bay during the Spanish-American War, paid him a very fine compliment indeed. Admiral George

Dewey said of him: "America never produced a navy officer more worthy of a place in history."

GIDEON WELLES

The summer of 1863 did indeed mark a turning point in the war. Although the Confederate forces remained strong, Lee's losses at Gettysburg and other equally important factors, such as the difficulty of replacing casualties with new recruits, made it impossible for the South to mount another major invasion of the North. The war had become largely a defensive action for the Confederacy, and the opposite for the Union.

The slow, steady weakening of the Confederacy led to the natural conclusion that the war would eventually end with a Union victory, and a public debate ensued in July 1863 pertaining to the issue of reconstruction. A split developed in the Republican party between moderates and radicals, the latter taking a decidedly hardline approach to what policies relating to the South should be implemented after the Union prevailed on the battlefield. Welles supported a moderate, fairly progressive approach to the issues under debate, backing Lincoln as he defended his policies of moderation against vocal and influential critics.

Welles had always held that the war was being fought against a rebellious people rather than rebellious states, an important distinction, because it maintained a strong conviction on his part to uphold the rights of individual states to determine their local government policies and functions with the least amount of federal interference. There were many who believed that because the eleven states in the Confederacy had seceded from the Union and waged war against it, they had forfeited any claim to state rights. This would open the defeated lands to the broad sweep of Federal law, and allow the federal government to reshape them into entities that would never again harm the collective welfare of the Union. This was to become increasingly important as time progressed, particularly after the war ended and the radical faction in the Republican party took control of the reconstruction process through Congress. Welles was unable to exert much influence on the outcome of the political process in Congress as it related to how the South was treated after the war. But under both Lincoln and Andrew Johnson he was at the forefront of the behind-the-scenes work in the executive branch to promote unity rather than revenge.

Most vexing at the time was the rather odd paradox that, through Lincoln's Emancipation Proclamation, slaves had been freed in the South but remained in bondage in loyal states. As a provision of readmittance into the Union, each Confederate state was forced to officially abolish slavery. Welles gave the constitutional problems with the situation and its various remedies much consideration, and ultimately agreed with Lincoln's belief that the only way to properly abolish slavery throughout the nation was through an amendment to the Constitution. This occurred with the ratification of the Thirteenth Amendment to the United States Constitution on December 6, 1865.

There was also the pressing matter of granting the vote to the freed slaves. On this, Welles revealed his elitist view of society and his adamant support of the right of a state to retain the power to shape its individual course in the context of the larger national identity at the expense of its disenfranchised black citizens. He did not support a Federal mandate to grant black suffrage, in part because of state rights issues, but also because he believed a mass of uneducated new voters would be an easy mark for "demagogues" and, thus, easily influenced to do the will of political manipulators. This would upset the delicate political elements at work in local governments in former Confederate states in their effort to put the pieces of the shattered social, political, and economic foundations of the region back together. While Welles never denied that the freed slaves should eventually have the right to vote, he was in no hurry to see it happen.

Congress did not directly address the issue of black suffrage until the ratification of the Fifteenth Amendment to the United States Constitution on February 3, 1870. The amendment did not specifically establish the mandate that all black male citizens should be entitled to vote. It simply stated that a qualified voter could not be denied the opportunity to cast a ballot based solely on race. Section One of this short amendment reads as follows:

The right of citizens of the United States to vote shall not be denied or abridged by the United States or by any state on account of race, color, or previous condition of servitude.

The Fourteenth Amendment, ratified on June 13, 1866, granted, among other things, citizenship for the freed slaves. This was a first step toward establishing civil rights for the black population as well as equal protection under the law, but it left unanswered the question of black suffrage. Welles was fully supportive of leaving the matter for resolution later, and as written the Fifteenth Amendment cohered to his view of state rights. The amendment left it up to the individual states to come up with the qualifications required for a black or white male to vote. (Women did not get the right to vote until the Nineteenth Amendment was ratified on August 18, 1920.) Thus, a very large loophole was open for abuse and the long, sad story of the struggle of African-Americans for equality in the political and social fabric of America would play out well into the twentieth century.

The period between 1861 and 1869, when he retired from public service, marked the most active years in Welles's political life. His administration of the Navy Department during the war was also a high point of his career, and he, along with his trusted assistants, contributed much to the Union's effort to stamp out the rebellion. His early and aggressive dedication to the development of steam-powered, armored warships was instrumental in fielding an effective fleet of vessels in the Monitor class. As the war progressed, he pushed hard for the development of fast, oceangoing armored cruisers to strengthen the United States against any attack by a foreign navy. His chief target of concern was Great Britain.

Welles presided over mistakes, such as the failed effort to build light draft Monitors, which proved ineffective. There were scandals and instances of fraud in the Navy Department. On the whole, however, it accomplished its mission to implement and enforce the blockade of more than 3,500 miles of coastline, and to attack coastal and river fortifications of the Confederacy, either on its own, or in combined land and sea offensives in conjunction with the War Department. He had taken the Navy from practically no ships to a vast force exceeding six hundred vessels, and just as effectively drew down the force to keep at its core a formidable nucleus of steam cruisers with veteran officers and sailors to man them.

After leaving Washington in 1869, Welles spent the remainder of his life with Mary in a comfortable home he purchased in Hartford. He contributed political editorials and essays to major newspapers and magazines, and wrote a book titled *Lincoln and Seward*, which was published in 1874. He had plans to write his memoirs, but never actually did. His letters and diaries, however, represent a comprehensive body of work valuable to any student of the nineteenth century in general, and the American Civil War in particular.

Welles died at home in 1878 at the age of seventy-five, after a short but painful illness. In the words of C. A. Dana, in *Recollections of the Civil War*, published in 1898: "There was nothing decorative about him; there was no noise in the street when he went along; but he understood his duty, and did it efficiently, continually, and unvaryingly."

THE OTHER RAIDERS

Of all the Confederate commerce destroyers, *Florida* and *Alabama* were the most famous, in part because of the charismatic and daring nature of their commanders. John Newland Maffitt and Raphael Semmes earned great acclaim in the Confederacy for their exploits. Both went on to write about their adventures after the war, preserving those exciting and dangerous days forever in the public record. There were six other raiders, however, and they deserve some mention, as do the privateers who preceded them. The demise of *Florida* and *Alabama* is also worthy of note.

Five days after the firing on Fort Sumter on April 12, 1861, the South offered to issue letters of marque to any owner of a vessel willing to arm her and prey upon the commerce of the United States. Thousands of applications were received in the spring of 1861, but only a small number of privateers actually set sail. They caused more alarm than damage, and most were quickly sunk. As the blockade improved in efficiency with the rapid expansion of the Union Navy, the profit potential for would-be privateers decreased and the risks increased. Most of the men engaged in the business turned to blockade running, which also became more hazardous as the war progressed. Nevertheless, enormous profits were made and a steady flow of war supplies, food, clothing, and other goods streamed into major Confederate ports such as Mobile, Charleston, and Wilmington. Large shipments of cotton flowed out of these same ports, most of it bound for Great Britain. Official Union estimates of the value of captured blockade runners and cargoes topped over $30 million. Not surprisingly, the majority of the prizes were British.

The fledgling Confederate Navy spent much time and money developing ironclads to fight on the inshore waters of the South, and it was somewhat successful. The Union, however, had a far greater ability to develop and construct ironclads because of its robust industrial base and substantial financial resources. It was not long before the Confederate Navy found itself outgunned on the rivers and sounds of its territory.

Many historians agree that the most successful use of Confederate assets in the naval arena was the deployment of its eight commerce raiders. These ships and crews accomplished much in the way of inflicting economic harm on the United States, as they literally swept the seas of most Yankee traders. Even as the handful of privateers were sailing northward on their hazardous voyages early in the war, Confederate agents were hard at work in Europe, intent upon purchasing or building fast, seaworthy vessels capable of long cruises to search for and destroy Union merchantmen. The Confederate Navy also sought ships at home that might work well as cruisers. The first raider of the war was *Sumter*, a refitted merchant vessel that sailed in 1861, under the command of Raphael Semmes. She took eighteen prizes before she was laid up in the spring of 1862 at Gibraltar.

The second commerce destroyer was *Nashville*, a sidewheel steamer seized in Charleston and converted into a raider. She sailed in the fall of 1861, and captured a prize off Ireland, making the port of Southampton, England on November 22. With the cooperation of the British, and in an obvious violation of international law governing the behavior of neutral nations, Nashville was allowed to go into dry dock for a major overhaul. Of further annoyance to officials in the United States, she was escorted to sea in January 1862 by a British gunboat while a pursuing Union warship was prohibited from taking up the chase until a mandatory twenty-four-hour waiting period elapsed.

In the case of the Union, the British were inclined to enforce all laws pertaining to the rights of belligerents in neutral ports. If a Union warship entered a harbor and found a Confederate vessel there, the Union captain could not wait for the Confederate to leave and steam after her as she departed. He had to wait an entire day. The same rights were supposedly applicable to a Union merchant vessel. If a Confederate raider showed up in a harbor and found a Union vessel there, the captain was obliged to give the potential prize a twenty-four-hour head start. Provisions also existed against lurking just off the harbor to await the emergence of a belligerent. In practice, though, there were many well-documented cases in which neutral governments ignored the twenty-four-hour rule in favor of the South.

Nashville escaped. She captured one ship on her way back to Confederate waters, where she was converted to a blockade runner, ending her career as a raider. *Sumter* and *Nashville* did not spend long on the high seas. However, the next two commerce destroyers, *Florida* and *Alabama*, stayed in service for an extended period. Both were commissioned in 1862 and saw action through most of 1864, racking up thirty-three and sixty-four prizes, respectively.

After turning away from the coast of New York in July 1863, too late to make his tentative rendezvous with Read, Maffitt sailed his cruiser across the Atlantic to Brest, France for a much needed refit. The sea had taken its toll on *Florida*. Her bottom was fouled with marine growth, her engines troubled with mechanical problems, and her crew ready for other duties. Almost two-thirds of them jumped ship in Brest, and agents in England were forced to send fresh hands to man her upon completion of the repairs in early 1864. The voyage and its travails had also taken a toll on Captain Maffitt. He was in such ill health that he requested, and was granted, a relief from the command. He returned to the South to skipper blockade runners, and proved immensely skillful at it, further bolstering his reputation as a Confederate patriot.

Florida set sail from France on February 10, 1864 under the command of Lieutenant Charles M. Morris. She was bound for the shipping lanes off Cape São Roque, where she and *Alabama* had caused such a panic the previous year. Upon arriving in the waters off Brazil, Morris noted the scarcity of Yankee vessels, so much so that he gave up searching for them and sailed for Bermuda, taking very few prizes in his long circuit of the Atlantic. Acting under orders from the Confederate Navy, he proceeded northward for another cruise to the New England coast and, on July 10, attacked four Yankee ships off the mouth of Chesapeake Bay. He discontinued his journey to New England, however, and turned southward to fit out in Brazil for a raid on the Union's Pacific whaling fleet. Unlike the merchant traders, the whalers remained relatively unharmed, though Semmes did attack some off the Azores on his maiden voyage from England.

Morris arrived at Bahia, Brazil on October 4, well after dark. The next morning, he and his crew awoke to find a formidable Union warship anchored nearby, the USS *Wachusett*. The commander of this ship was intent upon capturing *Florida* and her crew at any cost, including the total disregard of all points of international law that forbade any offensive action between belligerents inside a neutral port. While Morris and half his crew were ashore for the night, *Wachusett* got underway at three in the morning on October 7. She steamed right into *Florida*, hitting her with tremendous force. U.S. Marines fired on the crew, and the warship fired two of her biggest guns. Overwhelmed, the Confederate sailors surrendered. The Brazilians were furious, but did not stop *Wachusett* from towing the captured raider out of the harbor, bound for Hampton Roads.

The diplomatic uproar over the incident was extreme. The captain of *Wachusett* was court-martialed. The issue of what to do with *Florida* was decided on November 28,

1864, when a U.S. Army transport ship collided with the raider while she rode to her anchor in Hampton Roads, sending her to the bottom. Most historians agree that the collision was no accident, but rather an expeditious way to dispose of the raider and the attending diplomatic furor surrounding her.

The end of *Alabama* was far more dramatic, culminating in a battle after Semmes guided the raider on a cruise that took her over thousands of miles of open ocean for the better part of two years. She finished her first adventures in the summer of 1863 upon her departure from the waters off Brazil. She reached Cape Town in late July, sailed eastward into the Indian Ocean on a disappointing search for Yankee ships, and finally turned around and sailed for France, arriving in Cherbourg on June 11, 1864. The news of her presence in the harbor spread fast, and before long a Union warship, USS *Kearsarge*, steamed in to take a look at the Confederate raider. Unwilling to subject his ship to the twenty-four-hour rule, the captain promptly left and hovered off the coast just outside the three-league limit, thus keeping to international waters while he waited for *Alabama* to come out.

With the flair typical of the day, Semmes issued a challenge to his counterpart on board *Kearsarge*. It went through the Confederate agent in Cherbourg to the U.S. Consul, then on to Captain John Winslow at sea outside the harbor. In essence, it said, "I beg [*Kearsarge*] will not depart before I am ready to go out." Semmes recalled the victory over USS *Hatteras* in January 1863, and was obviously anxious for a repeat performance. Further, he found the mission of stalking and burning defenseless merchant ships rather boring as the months stretched to years. Winslow was equally anxious to fight Semmes. It would be a great boost to his career if he sank the most notorious raider on the sea.

The two ships engaged in a fierce battle on June 19, 1864, with thousands of French spectators gathered on shore to watch. The thunder of broadsides rolled across the water. Smoke obscured the combatants, then parted to reveal them firing at each other at close range. *Kearsarge* slowly pounded the raider to pieces, until she sank, stern first, beneath the waves. Sailors aboard a pleasure yacht sailing nearby to observe the action plucked Semmes out of the water, as well as some of his men, and took them to England, much to the consternation of the United States. French pilot boats rescued others. In all, out of a crew of 150, nine men aboard Alabama died in the battle, twenty-one were wounded, and ten drowned after the ship went down.

The fifth commerce destroyer, *Georgia*, was not well suited for the mission. Since she was built of iron, all major repairs required skilled workers in a shipyard. She also carried very little sail and thus relied almost solely on coal, always in limited supply. She was commissioned in April 1863, and for a time, she cruised the same waters off Brazil as *Florida* and *Alabama*, a very unpleasant consequence for Yankee merchantmen. In all, she took ten prizes before sailing to Cherbourg for repairs in the fall of 1863. She never went to sea as a raider again.

The sixth raider, *Rappahannock*, was purchased in the late fall of 1863. After putting to sea, her engines failed and she ran aground in France. She never saw any action.

The last two raiders put to sea late in the war, and did great damage to the U.S. merchant traders, as well as the whaling fleet. On July 20, 1864, *Tallahassee* was commissioned as a commerce destroyer and steamed from Wilmington north to New England. By the time she reached Halifax on August 18, she had taken more than forty prizes from New Jersey to Maine. Mindful of Read's demise in Portland, her captain stayed well offshore and did not attempt to raid any ports on the mainland. After narrowly escaping capture off Halifax, *Tallahassee* returned to the South. Her name was changed to *Olustee* and she went on another cruise, taking six prizes. In December 1864, she was converted to a blockade runner.

The last raider, *Shenandoah*, was dispatched to the Pacific to decimate the U.S. whaling fleet. She departed English waters in late October 1864, and over the next ten months sailed more than forty thousand miles and destroyed thirty-eight ships, most of them whalers. Her journey was epic in proportions, though it must have been quite monotonous for her crew. Her course took her south down the South Atlantic to the Cape of Good Hope into the Indian Ocean, where she followed the prevailing westerlies into the Pacific.

Shenandoah stopped in Australia in January 1865 to repair damage to the ship's propeller, then went on her way, reaching the waters of the Bering Sea in June 1865.

By now, of course, the war was over, but the captain did not believe it upon hearing the news. He continued his mission until recent newspapers from a captured prize convinced him that the Confederacy was gone. This occurred in early August. *Shenandoah* sailed all the way to England by way of Cape Horn, a distance of more than seventeen thousand miles, without stopping at any port. The captain and crew surrendered to the British upon arriving in Liverpool in November 1865.

Britain was eventually held accountable for its part in supporting the Confederate efforts to build and deploy commerce raiders. Of the eight cruisers deployed between 1861 and 1864, six were built in Great Britain, armed with British guns, and often were manned by British crewmen sympathetic to the Southern cause in spite of the provisions of the Foreign Enlistment Act. The United States took Britain to task for its role in building and arming the Confederacy's high seas raiders in what was known as the Alabama Claims case. It was heard at an international tribunal in Geneva in 1871.

The United States contended that Britain should be held financially responsible for the immense and adverse economic impact resulting from the raiders' actions. Damages were calculated, depending on the source, from $2.5 to close to $10 billion in 1870s currency in ships and cargoes lost; costs incurred to send U.S. ships to hunt for the cruisers; increased expenses for insurance on goods transported by sea; the devastating liability to merchants due to the transfer of U.S.-flagged ships to foreign owners out of desperate necessity; and even for the price in national treasure spent to prosecute the war subsequent to the battle of Gettysburg in July 1863. The British protested vehemently against such a broad-based spectrum of damages, and the international tribunal agreed that the Yanks had grossly overestimated the true costs. The Alabama Claims case was settled in 1872 when the United States was awarded $15.5 million in gold, a sum well below the actual economic losses.

APPENDIX

"The Florida's *Cruise"*

The following song was written by a sailor aboard *Florida* in April 1863, and was recorded in full in the diary of A. L. Drayton, who no doubt enjoyed it as the men sang in the forecastle. It is certainly not a work of literary excellence, but it reveals the spirit and perspective of the Confederates engaged in destroying Union merchant ships. It also contains mostly accurate details of the voyage up to the end of April. Drayton described the song as the "Red, White, and Blue, Southern Edition."

> One evening off Mobile the Yanks
> they all knew
> That the wind from the northard
> most billowy blew.

They also all knew and thought
    they were sure
That the *Florida* was blockaded,
    so safe so secure.

Nine cruisers they had and they
    lay off the bar through and through
Their line to seaward extended quite far.
And Preble said as he closed
    his eyes tight,
I am sure they are all hammocked
    this bitter cold night.

Bold Maffitt commanded, a man
    of great fame
Whose cruise in the Dolphin
    we've all heard of the same.
He called us all aft and these words
    he did say:
I'm bound to run out boys.
    Heave your anchor away.

Our hull was white washed,
    our sails were all stowed.
Our steam was chock up
    and a fresh wind it blowed.
As we crawled along by them,
    the Yanks gave a shout.
We dropped all our canvas
    and opened her out.

You would have thought them all mad
    if you heard the
Noise made upon seeing our flash
    little packet.
Their boatswains did pipe
    and the blue lights did play
While the great Drummond light,
    it turned night into day.

The Cuyler, a boat that's unrivalled
    for speed,
She quick let slip her cables
    very quickly indeed.
She thought for to catch us
    and keep us in prey
Till her larger companions
    could get underway.

She chased and chased
    until the dawning of day
Till she thought from her [?]
    she was too far away.
She gave up the chase
    and reported no doubt
That she had sunk us and burnt us
    somewhere there about.

Now we are out boys all on the salt sea.
We brought the Estelle to,
    right under our lee.

We burnt and sunk her with all
    her fine gear
And straight to Havana went the
    bold privateer.

There we recruited and took in some stores
And the [?] goodbye and set sail
    from their shore.
Before leaving their waters,
    by way of a joke,
With two Yankee brigs boys,
    we made a great smoke.

Our hull was well washed
    with limestone so white,
Which sailors all know is not
    gentle Christian-like.
So to paint her all ship shape
    we went to Green Keys
When the Sonoma [U.S. gunboat]
    came hoping the rebel to seize.

We made all sail and up steam
    right away
And for forty-eight hours she
    made us some play.
When our coal being dirty
    and choking the flue,
Our steam it slacked down
    and nearer she drew.

Oh ho! cries our Captain,
    I see what's your game,
So clear away your stern Pivot,
    the Bull dog, by name
And two small dogs to keep him company.
For very sharp teeth have these dogs
    of the sea.
    [The sailor is talking about the guns.]

The Sonoma came up until she
    was nearly in range
When her engines gave out,
    now wasn't that strange!
Now I don't know the truth
    but it's my firm belief
That she didn't like the looks
    of the Florida's teeth.

She gave up the chase and
    returned to Key West
And told the flag Captain that
    she had done her best.
But the story went round and grew
    rather strong
And the public acknowledged that
    something was wrong.

We went on a cruising and soon did espy
A fine lofty clipper coming home
    from Shanghai.

We burnt her and sunk her in the midst
of the sea
And drank to old Jeff in
the best of Bohea [a fine Chinese tea].

We next came to a ship with a Quakerish
name.
The wolf in sheep's clothing O plays
a deep game,
For in the hold of that beautiful
peaceable star
Was full of saltpetre to make powder
for war.

Of course the best nature never
could stand that.
Saltpetre for Boston was a little too fat.
So we burnt her and she made
a great blaze.
She's a mighty star now that never
will raise.

We next took a schooner well laden
with bread.
What the d—d got into old Uncle Abe's
head?
To send us such biscuit is such
a fine thing
That it sets us a laughing till we sit down
and sing.

We next took the Lapwing with the
    right stuff in her hold
And that was black diamonds
    that people call coal.
With that in our bunkers we'll tell
    Uncle Sam
That we think his gunboats are not
    worth a d—n.

The Colcord to Cape Town was bound.
We bade her heave to,
    and swing her yards round.
To Davy Jones Locker
    without further delay
we set her a fire and sailed on our way.

AUTHOR'S NOTE

Although Charles W. Read's rampage up the New England coast in 1863 remains obscure, it has not been completely ignored in articles and books from the late nineteenth century to the present. If one looks, it is possible to find a handful of secondary sources. For example, a rather good and accurate account appeared in the *Richmond Dispatch* in 1895, "Cruise of the Clarence, Tacony — Archer." A particularly terrible account appeared in *Munsey's Magazine* in 1916, Walter Scott Meriwether's "The Paul Jones of the Confederacy." The article was published as nonfiction, but it contained so many errors and embellishments of fact that any future researchers who may consult it should take it as fiction.

Therein lay the root of the problem when I set out to research Read's adventure. As the authors before me, with some exceptions, wrote their versions of the events, it seems they copied each other and loaded the secondary record with events that appear never to have occurred. Few readers will go back to research the original record, nor should they feel compelled to do so, unless they are engaged in a project such as this one. Thus, the reader would not be able to readily identify cases of fiction mingled in with fact, as I was able to by mustering all the sources I could find to flesh out the details of the story that had captured my imagination. It was frustrating to the point where I discounted every secondary source, in spite of the loss of some great copy. I will provide a few examples of this great copy to illustrate what I mean and to show how I decided to respond.

On June 11, as *Clarence* was sailing westward toward the mouth of Chesapeake Bay, various secondary sources indicate that a Union gunboat forced the raider to heave to and boarded her with a party of ten armed sailors. Read supposedly was able to place all the Quaker guns below decks before the boarding party arrived, quite an unlikely feat, given the weight and number of the wooden guns and the length of time it would have taken to hoist them into the hold. Read also supposedly told one of his men to update the logbook. When the Union officer was escorted to the captain's cabin to view the ship's papers, he was deceived. The story even goes so far as to assert that Read recognized the officer as a former classmate from Annapolis while they sipped sherry together in the cabin, but that the officer failed to recognize him because he had a sou'wester hat pulled low over his face. The Union officer left, sending *Clarence* on her way without further interference.

At first glance, the deception appeared to fit Read's character. The problem was no firsthand account mentioned it. There were prisoners aboard *Clarence*. One of them stated in the press that a Union warship came near the raider and that guns were thrown overboard out of fear of being discovered. He said nothing about a boarding. More important, Confederate sailor A. L. Drayton failed to mention the boarding or the heaving of guns overboard. He only said a ship thought to be a Union gunboat drew near enough to frighten the crew on the evening of June 11. Certainly he would have been involved in heaving guns overboard, and would definitely have noted the boarding. The account of the prisoner in the press regarding the guns may have been the result of disinformation fed to him by Read and his men. At any rate, Drayton's journal was one of the most important primary sources I used to sort fact from fiction, and to bring the voyage into full relief within the narrative. He wrote pages detailing all that occurred aboard *Clarence*, *Tacony*, and *Archer*. In short, I trusted him above any secondary or contemporary source.

On at least two occasions, it was said that Union warships hove *Tacony* to during the great hunt that ensued after news of the attack off *Chesapeake* Bay hit Washington. Read was said to have pretended to be a Union merchantman and to have shouted over to the Union officers aboard the gunboats that he had seen a few hours past the very raider they were searching for, and promptly sent them off to chase their tails. As in the previous case, neither Read nor Drayton mentioned these incidents. Did they occur? Perhaps. But I think not.

Then there was the issue with the Dutch cheese. Off Portland, Maine, as the Union steamboats closed in with *Caleb Cushing* and Read's men ran out of shot for the cannon, it was said that First Officer Brown went below and came back topsides with an old Dutch cheese. As absurd as it sounds, the rebels supposedly loaded the cheese into the cannon and shot the steamer *Chesapeake* with it, scoring the only direct hit of the short exchange of cannon fire. The Union soldiers and citizen volunteers aboard the steamer were said to have screamed something to the effect of "They're firing stink bombs at us!"

Not one official record, nor the private journal of John Mead Gould, who was an eyewitness aboard *Chesapeake*, nor the reporter from the *Eastern Argus*, who was also aboard the steamer, said anything about being hit with a cheese. Here was one instance of "great copy" I felt no compulsion to insert. The decision not to include the cheese was easy, since it was so farfetched. I rather doubt Read's men would have fired a cheese at anybody, much less an approaching ship full of armed Yankees. The record clearly establishes, based on eyewitness accounts as well as Read's testimony to reporters, that the rebels indeed fired bits of iron, nails, stones, and other items toward the end of the engagement.

Dramatic events make great stories, and the ones that are most compelling often acquire cargoes of myths to transform reality into legend. Such was the case with Charles W. Read. However, after a thorough study of official records, reports from eyewitnesses published in the press, and the private journals of those who were involved, I found plenty of excitement to fill the pages of this narrative while retaining a solid command of the facts and events as they really occurred. The following primary sources proved to be the most valuable: Department of the Navy, *Official Records of the Union and Confederate Navies of the War of the Rebellion*; the Diary of A. L. Drayton; Log of the *Tacony*; and the Diary of Gideon Welles. Welles's diary is a must-read for anyone interested in a comprehensive, firsthand account of the behind-the-scenes workings of Lincoln's cabinet. I found it quite fascinating. It revealed much about the cool-headed Connecticut Yankee who contributed so much to the war effort.

BIBLIOGRAPHY

PRIMARY SOURCES

Department of the Navy. *Official Records of the Union and Confederate Navies of the War of the Rebellion, Series 1, Volume 2, Operations of the Cruisers.* Washington, DC: Government Printing Office, 1895.

Drayton, A. L. Diary, January–June 1863. Washington, DC: Library of Congress, Manuscripts Division.

Gift, George W. "The Story of the Arkansas." *Southern Historical Society Papers,* Vol. 12, Richmond, VA, 1884.

Gould, John Mead. *The Civil War Journals of John Mead Gould 1861–1866.* Edited by William B. Jordan, Jr. Baltimore: Butternut and Blue, 1997.

Log of the Bark Tacony. Washington, DC: National Archives and Record Administration, Record Group 45.

Read, Charles W. "Reminiscences of the Confederate States Navy," *Southern Historical Society Papers*, Vol. 2, no. 5, 1876.

Contemporary Sources and Related Articles

Hale, Clarence. "The Capture of the Caleb Cushing." *Collections of the Maine Historical Society*, series 3, volume 1. Portland, ME: 1904.

Meriwether, Walter Scott. "The Paul Jones of the Confederacy," *Munsey's Magazine*, July 1916.

Monthly Record of Current Events, *Harper's New Monthly Magazine*, June to November 1863, 415.

New York Times, New York Tribune, New York Herald, Eastern Argus, and others, from 1861 through the summer of 1863.

Wood, Robert H. "Cruise of the Clarence, Tacony — Archer" *Richmond Dispatch*, Sunday, November 24, 1895.

Books

Boswell, Charles. *The America: The Story of the World's Most Famous Yacht*. New York: David McKay Company, 1967.

Boykin, Edward. *Sea Devil of the Confederacy: The Story of the Florida and her Captain, John Newland Maffitt*. New York: Funk & Wagnalls Company, 1959.

Campbell, Thomas R. *Sea Hawk of the Confederacy: Lt. Charles W. Read and the Confederate Navy*. Shippensburg, PA: Burd Street Press, 2000.

Commager, Henry Steele. *The Blue and the Gray*. New York: Crescent Books, 1995.

Donald, David Herbert. *Lincoln*. New York: Simon & Schuster, 1995.

Editors. *Echoes of Glory: Illustrated Atlas of the Civil War*. Alexandria, VA: Time-Life Books, 1991.

Foote, Shelby. *The Civil War: A Narrative* (three volumes). New York: Vintage Books, 1986.

Franklin, John Hope. *The Emancipation Proclamation*. New York: Doubleday & Company, 1963.

Jones, Robert A. *Confederate Corsair: The Life of Lt. Charles W. "Savez" Read*. Mechanicsburg, PA: Stackpole Books, 2000.

Jones, Virgil Carrington. *The Civil War at Sea* (three volumes). New York: Holt, Rinehart, Winston, 1960.

Leech, Margaret. *Reveille in Washington 1860–1865*. New York: Harper & Brothers Publishers, 1941.

Maffitt, Emma M. *The Life and Services of John Newland Maffitt*. New York: The Neale Publishing Company, 1906.

Malone, Dumas. *Dictionary of American Biography*. New York: Charles Scribner's Sons, 1935 [1963].

McPherson, James M., and Patricia R. McPherson. *Lamson of the* Gettysburg: *The Civil War Letters of Lieutenant Roswell H. Lamson, U.S. Navy*. New York: Oxford University Press, 1997.

Musicant, Ivan. *Divided Waters: The Naval History of the Civil War*. New York: HarperCollins Publishers, 1995.

Niven, John. *Gideon Welles: Lincoln's Secretary of the Navy*. New York: Oxford University Press, 1973.

Ploski, Harry A., and Ernest Kaiser, ed. *The Negro Almanac*. New York: The Bellwether Company, 1971.

Smith, Mason Philip. *Confederates Downeast*. Portland, ME: The Provincial Press, 1985.

Stern, Philip Van Doren. *The Confederate Navy: A Pictorial History*. New York: Doubleday & Company: 1962.

Thompson, Robert Means, and Richard

Wainwright, eds. *Confidential Correspondence of Gustavus Vasa Fox*. New York: The Naval History Society, 1920.

Welles, Gideon. *Diary of Gideon Welles: Secretary of the Navy Under Lincoln and Johnson*. Volume 1, 1861 — March 30, 1864. New York: Houghton Mifflin Company, 1911.

West, Richard S., Jr. *Gideon Welles: Lincoln's Navy Department*. New York: The Bobbs-Merrill Company, 1943.

West, Richard S., Jr. *Mr. Lincoln's Navy*. New York: Longman, Green and Company, 1957.

Williams, H. Dwight. *A Year in China: and a Narrative of Capture and Imprisonment, When Homeward Bound, On Board the Rebel Pirate* Florida. New York: Hurd and Houghton, 1864.

ACKNOWLEDGMENTS

The process of researching and writing narrative nonfiction requires undivided attention to detail, and a dedication to finding the best way to tell the story while remaining true to the facts. Often, the latter part of the enterprise offers discoveries and surprises similar to those that a fiction writer must experience as the narrative moves forward on its own momentum. With the right material to work with, the characters take over and the author simply comes along for the ride. One thing is certain: The process cannot be forced. It has to come as naturally as breathing.

However, there is more to writing than that. For a book to find its own way in the world it needs more than an author to make it so. A large team of players enter into the equation — publishers, editors, agents, publicists, sales representatives, booksellers, reviewers, and, most important, the readers. All are essential.

My wife, Elizabeth, a real history buff, was truly inspirational in her excitement for the story. Sometimes, when the going gets tough, it is vital to have a person to talk with about the seemingly small details.

My agent, Jill Grinberg, and my editors at the Free Press, Andrea Au and Fred Hills, all offered insightful comments and suggestions that helped improve the manuscript in its early drafts. They are valued partners in my efforts as an author, and I am lucky to have such skilled and dedicated people on my team.

The number of archivists and librarians who helped me during my research, both for the text and for the selection of images contained in the book are too numerous to mention, but they all have my thanks and gratitude. Without a good reference librarian or an archivist with intimate knowledge of the resources within a given collection of rare manuscripts or photographs, my work would be impossible. While an author may spend most of his or her time alone, there are no doubt a goodly number of people involved in the effort at hand, ready to provide the help that is needed for the book to take wing and fly. My thanks to everyone who helped me with this one.

ABOUT THE AUTHOR

A journalist for nearly twenty years, author DAVID W. SHAW has written extensively about nineteenth-century American history in four of his previous books. His most recent is *America's Victory*, a riveting account of the world's most famous yacht race, held in 1851, which led to the establishment of the America's Cup, the oldest international trophy in competitive sports. Shaw's expertise as a sailor and his in-depth knowledge of the Civil War make him ideally suited to tell the story of Confederate raider Charles W. Read and his voyage of 1863. Shaw has contributed articles to numerous publications, including the *New York Times*, *Entrepreneur*, *Woman's World*, and *New Jersey Monthly*.